FLAVOURS SERIES

Apples

Elaine Elliot & Virginia Lee

Formac Publishing Company Limited
Halifax

In continuing the theme of the Flavours series of cookbooks, we have invited chefs from across Canada to share their recipes, and we thank them for their generosity. Each recipe has been tested and adjusted for the home cook.   — Elaine Elliot and Virginia Lee

Special thanks to **Craig Flinn**, chef and proprietor of Chives Canadian Bistro in Halifax, for preparing and styling many of the recipes photographed for this book.

Participating restaurants

British Columbia
Bishop's Restaurant, Vancouver, BC
Castle on the Mountain Bed & Breakfast, Vernon, BC
Cobble House Bed & Breakfast, Cobble Hill, BC
Qualicum Bay Bed & Breakfast, Qualicum Beach, BC
Quattro on Fourth, Vancouver, BC
Sequoia Grill at the Teahouse, Vancouver, BC
Alberta
Pyramid Lake Resort, Jasper, AB
River Café Island Park, Calgary, AB
Manitoba
Current Restaurant at Inn at the Forks, Winnipeg, MB
Ontario
Beild House, Collingwood, ON
Deerhurst Resort, Huntsville, ON
Hillebrand Estates Winery Restaurant, Niagara-on-the-Lake, ON
Inn on the Twenty, Jordon, ON
Oban Inn, Niagara-on-the-Lake, ON
Ste. Anne's Country Inn and Spa, Grafton, ON
Wellington Court Restaurant, St. Catharines, ON
Westover Inn, St. Marys, ON
Quebec
Château Bonne Entente, Sainte Foy, QC
Restaurant Les Fougères, Chelsea, QC

New Brunswick
A. Hiram Walker Estate Heritage Inn, St. Andrews, NB
Quaco Inn, St. Martins, NB
San Martello Dining Room at Dufferin Inn & Suites, Saint John, NB
Prince Edward Island
Dalvay-by-the-Sea, Dalvay, PE
The Dunes Cafe and Gardens, Brackley Beach, PE
Inn at Bay Fortune, Bay Fortune, PE
Inn at Spry Point, Spry Point, P
Nova Scotia
Acton's Grill & Cafe, Wolfville, NS
Blomidon Inn, Wolfville, NS
Chives Canadian Bistro, Halifax, NS
Duncreigan Country Inn, Mabou, NS
Evangeline Café, Grand Pre, NS
Gowrie House Country Inn, Sydney Mines, NS
Inn on the Lake, Waverley, NS
Keltic Lodge, Ingonish Beach, NS
La Perla, Dartmouth, NS
Liscombe Lodge, Liscomb, NS
Mountain Gap Inn and Resort, Smiths Cove, NS
Nemo's Restaurant, Halifax, NS
Newfoundland
Gaffer's Gourmet Bistro at Whitehall Country Inn, Clarenville, NL

Formac Publishing Company Limited recognizes the support of the Province of Nova Scotia through the Department of Tourism, Culture and Heritage. We acknowledge the financial support of the Government of Canada through the Book Publishing Industry Development Program (BPIDP) for our publishing activities.

Formac Publishing Company Limited
5502 Atlantic Street
Halifax, Nova Scotia B3H 1G4
www.formac.ca

Library and Archives Canada Cataloguing in Publication

Elliot, Elaine, 1939-
        Apples : recipes from Canada's best chefs / Elaine Elliot and Virginia Lee. -- 2nd ed.

(Flavours series)
Includes index.
ISBN10: 0-88780-698-8
ISBN13: 978-0-88780-698-8

        1. Cookery (Apples) 2. Cookery, Canadian. I. Lee, Virginia, 1947-
II. Title. III. Series.

TX813.A6E453 2006   641.6'411   C2006-904337-X

Printed and bound in Canada

Contents

Introduction

The first domesticated apples were introduced into Nova Scotia shortly after Samuel de Champlain established the settlement of Port Royal in 1605, from seed brought from France. Most early farms had their own orchard. The climate and soil proved so favourable that the 1698 census listed 1,584 apple trees at Port Royal. The trees planted from seed in the New World eventually reverted to the wild and crossed with crabapples, the only apples native to North America.

During the 17th and 18th centuries apple orchards were established by both English and French colonists. Apples were an important part of the settlers' diet. They were eaten fresh, or dried for use in pies, puddings and sauces throughout the year; those not fit for eating were fed to the pigs. Apples were pressed into cider — a safe alternative to drinking water that was often contaminated by livestock.

As pioneers headed west they found that the prairies were too cold and dry to grow apples. On the West Coast the opposite problems were faced: too warm, too wet. Settlers soon discovered that mountain valleys provided the cooler temperatures needed for apple growing.

Early settlers lacked the knowledge of grafting, much of which had been lost during the Middle Ages. The process of grafting, by which domesticated apples are propagated, was described in Greek writings from the 3rd century BCE. The knowledge gradually spread across the Mediterranean and made its way to Britain with the Romans.

For a couple of hundred years during the Middle Ages, apples fell out of favour with the poorer classes and various ills were attributed to the fruit. The apple's reputation was further sullied when the King James Bible, printed on the newly invented printing press, named the forbidden fruit "apple" for the first time. Nonetheless, apples continued to be popular among the upper classes and soon regained universal favour. As with so much other learning, the monasteries kept the craft of grafting alive for future generations and in the 19th century, apple varieties proliferated.

Apple growing began to emerge as an important industry in the mid-1800s. It takes 15 to 20 years to develop a new apple and by the 1940s, there were more than 1,000 named varieties from which to choose. Market demands for perfect-looking apples that kept well dictated the demise of many old varieties; among them were many wonderful-tasting apples that have become extinct.

Some of the best early varieties of apples were discovered more by accident than design. John McIntosh, a settler in Upper Canada (Ontario), found a particularly tasty apple in an overgrown orchard on his land. His early attempts at grafting failed, but in 1835 an itinerant peddler showed him the proper method. Millions of apple trees populating the orchards of North America descended from that one tree and the McIntosh became Canada's signature apple.

Apples will not grow just anywhere. They have very specific soil and climatic requirements: deep, well-drained soil and moderate winter weather; warm days and cool nights. Orchard sites must be frost-free for 120–145 days and have some shelter from the wind. Apples need a period of at least two months' dormancy brought on by sub-zero (or very close to zero) temperatures. Areas of good soil where temperatures are moderated by water (the East and West coasts and around the Great Lakes) are good apple-growing sites. Shelter may be provided by mountains or valleys. Thus in Nova Scotia, the apple industry is centred in the Annapolis Valley, and in New Brunswick along the Saint John River Valley. Quebec has mountains that offer protection along the north shore of the St. Lawrence River. In Ontario, orchards thrive around Georgian Bay and in the Niagara Peninsula.

The Prairie Provinces are generally too cold for commercial apple production, although some hardy varieties were developed in the 20th century at the Canadian Department of Agriculture site in Morden, MB. The mountains of Alberta offer protection for the growing of limited varieties of apples. In British Columbia, the introduction of artificial irrigation to the Okanagan Valley rendered it a prime fruit-growing area. Apples are also cultivated in the Fraser Valley.

Having the right site is just the beginning. Starting and maintaining an apple orchard is an expensive, labour-intensive and risky business.

A successful orchardist must be a farmer, a scientist and a marketer.

Apples have a long and complex genetic history. If you plant seeds from, say, a McIntosh apple, the fruits of the resultant trees will not be Macs, nor will they be like one another. In fact you would probably get as many different varieties as seeds planted. Apple varieties are not reproduced by seed, but by cloning using a method called grafting. Every cultivated apple tree is a combination of the best of two trees. Grafting is the process of binding a shoot cut from a tree that produces good apples into a notch cut on a rootstock tree which was bred for cold hardiness, disease resistance, size and suitability to particular soil conditions. The grafted cutting, or scion, determines the variety of fruit the tree will bear and is chosen for taste, appearance and marketability.

To further complicate the issue, apple trees are cross-pollinators (i.e., they need to be fertilized by a different variety). A McIntosh fertilized with pollen from a Spartan will produce not a hybrid as might be expected, but true Macs. To get an abundance of apples, an orchard must be planted with at least two varieties. Beehives are often placed in orchards to encourage cross-pollination.

Size is an important factor in the selection of trees. Apple trees come in three sizes — standard, semi-dwarf and dwarf. Old-fashioned trees are all standard, newer trees are dwarf or semi-dwarf. The useful life of standard trees is twice as long as dwarfs and they bear about three times as much fruit. However, standard trees require more space, they grow too tall to be pruned, sprayed and harvested from the ground, and maintenance is expensive and inefficient. Dwarf trees bear fruit sooner (three to six years) than standards (eight years), and maintenance and harvesting are easier and more economical. Dwarfs are a good choice for growers with limited acreage or for the home grower.

The orchardist has a huge vested interest in the health of his trees. Healthy trees live longer and bear more and better fruit. Although apple trees are relatively easy to grow, they are susceptible to

several diseases and damaging insects. Growers must be up to date on the latest, most effective and most environmentally responsible methods of combatting disease and pests.

Apple trees require annual pruning. A tree's upward growth must be controlled, the number of side branches is restricted to improve productivity and the centre of the tree must be kept open to air circulation and sunlight. Damaged boughs must be removed to prevent disease.

Harvesting takes place from late August through October. Apples are picked when they are fully ripe (but not too ripe). You should always be able to eat an apple straight from the tree. An experienced orchardist will know when

the time is right by looking at the crop. For the novice, the proof is in the seeds. If they are dark, the apple is ripe for the picking. Apples for the fresh market are picked by hand to avoid bruising and emptied (carefully) into wooden bins to be trucked to storage and packing facilities.

Packing companies inspect and grade the apples and pack them in plastic bags or trayed in boxes for either bulk or individual sale. They are then either stored or transported to market by truck or, in the case of off-shore markets, by boat.

Apples are graded in Canada under the Canada Agricultural Products Act by colour, uniformity of size (a minimum diameter of 5.7

cm or 2.2 in) and quality (freedom from disease, defects and damage, and cleanliness) as Canada Extra Fancy, Canada Fancy and Canada Commercial. Apples are also pressure-tested for firmness to establish internal quality. Some provinces also have their own grading standards, for example, B.C. Extra Fancy. Commercial or "C" grade apples may have less colour than Canada Fancy or they may have irregular shapes or slight cosmetic defects, none of which affect the flavour. These apples are excellent for cooking.

A pivotal factor in the growth of the apple industry has been advancements in methods of storage. Apples begin to deteriorate as soon as they are picked. Apples breathe and they continue to breathe (and to ripen) as long as they are exposed to oxygen. Ideally, apples should be kept as cold as possible without freezing. This slows respiration and delays deterioration. Humidity also has a bearing on the rate of deterioration, and storage in a controlled humidity of more than 85% prevents loss of moisture by evaporation.

In olden days, farmers found that apples packed in barrels and buried underground kept longer than if they were left in the open air. This somewhat primitive method did the job to a certain extent. The root cellar soon became a part of every farm and provided a more palatable method of delaying deterioration. Research in the 1920s led to the construction of the first cold storage units in Canada. Apples were chilled to 0°C in special chambers and humidity was kept at 85%. Apples kept in cold storage will remain fresh for up to six months. Cold storage was a boon to the industry and is still used today for shorter-term storage.

By the 1950s, research began in Canada on a more sophisticated storage method called controlled atmosphere storage or CA. This new technique combined airtight refrigeration at 0°C with decreased oxygen and increased carbon dioxide. Apples can be kept in CA storage longer than under cold storage — in some cases up to a year. The caveat is that fruit has to be of the highest quality and the storage must be filled and sealed quickly for the process to work well.

Farmers no longer had to sell all their apples in a couple of months, and it was now possible for consumers to buy fresh apples throughout the winter months. More varieties of apples became available for most of the year at reasonable prices.

Apples are Canada's largest tree fruit crop. Approximately 400,000 tonnes of apples, worth over $160 million, are grown annually. (Figures fluctuate from year to year due to variations in climate and market conditions.) Ontario is the largest producer of apples in Canada, followed by British Columbia. Fresh apples account for about two-thirds of all apple sales. The rest are processed for juice and cider and for canning or baking.

Most apple processing in Canada is in the hands of a few companies. One of these, Lassonde Industries Inc., a Quebec-based company founded in 1918 as a vegetable canning facility, expanded its operation in 1959 to produce apple juice. Today its subsidiary, A. Lassonde Inc., has a network of half a dozen plants in Canada for apple storage and production. Using modern equipment and technology, it has become one of the leading apple processors in Eastern Canada. Lassonde sells juices and fruit drinks under many recognized labels such as Allen's, Everfresh, Fruité and Oasis. Lassonde also has operations in the United States and in about 20 countries worldwide.

In 1991, Lassonde expanded into Nova Scotia with the acquisition of Greatvalley Juices in Port Williams in the Annapolis Valley. Greatvalley produces apple juice and other fruit drinks under the familiar brand names Graves, Avon and Nature's Best, and is the major supplier to grocery wholesalers in the Atlantic region.

In 2002, Lassonde acquired Golden Town Apple Products near Thornbury in Ontario's apple-growing region on Georgian Bay. Golden Town is the largest buyer of processing apples in Ontario (50,000 tonnes of apples annually) and one of the top three apple processors in Canada. Formerly P. Haines & Son, founded in 1906, it is one of the oldest extant apple-processing companies in Canada. Golden Town supplies Ontario and United States markets with

fresh and frozen apple slices as well as pure juice. The company's success is based on using high-quality apples processed under optimum conditions and delivered quickly to customers.

British Columbia produces one-third of all apples grown in Canada. Sun-Rype Products Ltd. is the main apple processor in British Columbia. Based in Kelowna, in the heart of the Okanagan Valley, it produces pure apple juice, fruit beverages and fruit snacks. Sun-Rype processes 30,000 to 60,000 tonnes of apples a year and supplies markets across Canada.

There are the few big players and then there are the many small local apple processors. Many farms, often in tandem with U-pick operations, produce their own sweet or hard apple cider and specialty vinegars and wines that are sold on-site at roadside markets or distributed locally. These, though not significant in terms of apple industry figures, are part of the culture and fabric of Canada.

Canada exports apples worth over $50 million a year to more than 20 countries. The United States, Mexico and the United Kingdom are the biggest markets; markets in Europe and the Caribbean are smaller and inconsistent, and traditional markets in the Asia Pacific region have recently been lost to China, one of the biggest apple producers in the world.

In recent years, Canada's apple industry has faced a number of challenges. Capital investment is enormous. Production costs have escalated. Competition has become stiff. Increased production worldwide has led to lower prices for Canadian growers. Growers have invested heavily in planting new cultivars that are now so widely available that prices have dropped. Canada has lost some of its traditional markets to countries now producing large quantities of apples at low prices. Canadian apples must compete for space in the supermarket with apple imports from the United States, New Zealand and Australia, with traditional fruits such as bananas and citrus, and with the many exotic fruits from around the world that are now available year-round.

Canada has responded to the challenges by striving to produce not the most, not the cheapest, but the best apples. Canadian apples, in fact all Canadian agricultural products, are the safest in the world. Consumers today are very knowledgeable about nutrition and environmental concerns, demanding foods that are safe and nutritionally sound. Canada's growers, with the help of government agencies, are working to produce apples that will fill that niche. Toward this end, growers are engaging in good agricultural management practices to address environmental concerns and to reduce costs and pesticide usage.

Canada's growers use fewer pesticides than many other countries and are trying to improve on that record. An Integrated Pest Management Strategy has been developed to help growers minimize the use of pesticides and maximize their effectiveness. Scientists are working to find alternative ways to control pests and disease. Integrated Fruit Production (IFP) guidelines are being developed and implemented. IFP is defined as the economical production of high-quality fruit that gives priority to ecologically sound methods, and minimizes the use of agricultural chemicals, thereby protecting the environment and human health.

In the 21st century, Canada is a world leader in producing, storing and processing apples in innovative and environmentally responsible ways. Canada continues to be an important player in the world market and provides the domestic market with fresh, high-quality, safe apples almost year-round.

Two governmental departments regulate and support the apple industry. The Canadian Food Inspection Agency concerns itself with food safety, quality issues and plant health. Agriculture and Agri-Food Canada provides producers with market information, market development, research and financial support.

There are about 20,000 kinds of apples in the world. Some 8,000 varieties have been bred, but only 20 or so varieties of apples are grown commercially in Canada, and maybe half a dozen favourites dominate the market. Old varieties are being replaced by newer hybrids to meet consumer demands for perfect-looking apples year-round. For example, in Nova Scotia the McIntosh, for many years Canada's most popular export, is being replaced by Honeycrisp. The perfect apple that

consumers seek and that growers strive to supply is firm, crisp and flavourful.

Roadside stands are a traditional source of fresh apples and many apple orchards have U-pick operations. The taste of an apple plucked from the tree on a sunny fall day is the best! But today you don't really have to go to the country to get good-quality "fresh" apples. They are as near as the local supermarket.

Fresh apples add crunch and colour to salads and complement cheese trays. On Hallowe'en, the most popular house on the block is the one where taffy apples are shelled out as treats. Fresh apples float — they are 25% air — and bobbing for apples is hilarious fun at fall parties. Apples are the main ingredient in many desserts, including old favourites such as apple pie, apple

crisp, apple strudel and baked apple. About one-third of the apples grown in Canada are processed into products such as pasteurized juice, dried apples, sliced apples, applesauce, cider (fresh or fermented), vinegar and wine. Juice is by far the most important apple product.

Remember when you used to take an apple to school for recess? Well, it turns out our mothers knew a thing or two. An apple is a great snack — handy and tasty, as well as nutritious. One medium apple has about 100 calories and 24 grams of carbohydrate for instant energy. It is a good source of vitamin C, providing 15% of the recommended daily intake, an excellent source of dietary fibre, at 4.3 grams, and it provides all the potassium you need. It contains no salt and a negligible amount of fat. Increased consumer awareness of the health benefits of eating apples has contributed to an increase in consumption in recent years.

Researchers have long known that apples (especially the skins) are a good source of antioxidants, a group of phytochemicals that scavenge and neutralize unstable molecules called free radicals. Free radicals, which can wreak havoc on cells and tissues, are believed to play a role in the onset of heart disease, stroke, diabetes, and prostate, colon and other cancers.

Look for firm, well-shaped, smooth-skinned fruit with rich even colour according to variety, free of bruises and wrinkles. Brownish freckled skin does not affect flavour.

The length of time apples will keep after purchase depends on the variety and can range from one to several months. In general, apples love to be cool; in fact, they soften ten times faster at room temperature. To keep apples at home, put unwashed fruit in a plastic bag, punch a few holes in the bag and refrigerate at about 41°F/4°C. Discard any bruised, damaged or soft apples. If they are left in the bag they will give off ethylene gas, causing nearby apples to spoil. Remember the old adage about the bad apple?

To prepare, just rinse and eat. To prevent browning of sliced or chopped apples, quickly brush cut surfaces with lemon or other citrus juice. Apple flesh begins to discolour as soon as it is exposed to air.

Innkeepers and restaurant chefs take full advantage of this beautiful, nutritious fruit. They offer new takes on old favourites. They also use apples in unique and innovative desserts, salads and main-course dishes.

In many instances, the chefs have specified the variety of apple to be used in their recipes. These suggestions obviously reflect the varieties grown in their particular region. Ontario chefs favour Crispins, Northern Spys or Cortlands, while British Columbia chefs are partial to Ambrosias or Granny Smiths. Gravensteins and McIntosh are the overall favourites of Maritime chefs. If a suggested variety is unavailable, you can safely substitute another variety with similar characteristics.

Apples have it all! In a fruit you cannot do better for taste, versatility, economy, nutrition and visual appeal than the apple. We in Canada have tended to take our apples for granted but look at them again; sample new cultivars as well as traditional varieties. Even if Ben Franklin's prescription of "An apple a day keeps the doctor away" does not offer a guarantee of eternal health, we suggest an apple a day just for the pure enjoyment of it. May this book enhance your appreciation of our wonderful Canadian apples!

Apple Varieties

Ambrosia
This cone-shaped medium-to-large red apple has a creamy yellow striping and is a favourite of British Columbian growers. An excellent snacking apple, the Ambrosia should be used within four months of harvest. Juicy and aromatic, it is slow to discolour when peeled, making it an ideal apple for salads.

Braeburn
Available late October to June. An old-fashioned medium-to-large apple with red skin. Flesh is yellowish to cream, juicy and crisp. Good for baking, fresh eating, salads and juice. Grown in British Columbia.

Cortland
Available early October to May. A medium-to-large apple with shiny bright red skin and greenish yellow stripes. The white flesh is slow to discolour. Excellent for eating fresh, in salads and applesauce. Good for pies, baking whole and freezing. Grown from Ontario east to the Maritimes.

Crabapple
Available late September to late November. While not a true member of Malus domestica, this small, hard, yellow-to-red fruit should be mentioned because it makes wonderful jelly and pickled garnish.

Crispin
Originally developed in Japan as Mutsu, this greenish-yellow apple with an orange blush is harvested in October and is available year round. Noted for its sweet yet refreshing taste, it is an excellent choice for eating, baking and juice production. Crispins are grown in Ontario.

Empire
Available mid-October to June. Hybrid of Red Delicious and McIntosh. Medium-red on yellow or all-red skin, slightly sweet and spicy, crisp and juicy. Store well, excellent fresh eating, poor for salads, applesauce, pies, baking whole and freezing. Grown in British Columbia, Ontario, Quebec and Nova Scotia.

Fuji
Available mid-October to June. Developed in Japan in 1939, the Fuji is a medium to large apple with yellowish green skin and red-orange highlights. Firm, sweetly tart, juicy and crisp. Retains its flavour even when held in lengthy storage. Excellent for salads, baking and sauce. Grown in British Columbia.

Gala
Available mid-August to December. Medium-sized with red striping over yellow-gold skin. Flesh is creamy yellow, semi-sweet, crisp and juicy. Excellent for fresh eating, in salads and served with soft, mild cheeses. Good for baking and sauce. Grown in British Columbia and Ontario.

Golden Delicious
An excellent all-purpose apple, this yellow or greenish-yellow variety is crisp when harvested but doesn't store well. Available from late September through June, the Golden Delicious has a mild, sweet flavour making it good for eating, fresh desserts and salads, baking and freezing. Grown in British Columbia and Ontario.

Golden Russet
Available November to May. Small round apple with rough golden brown skin and creamy juicy flesh. Excellent fresh eating apple with a superior storage life. Poor for salads, applesauce, pies, baking whole and freezing. Grown in Ontario, Quebec and New Brunswick.

Granny Smith

Very popular import available year-round. Round medium-sized fruit with green skin. White flesh, firm and tart, but sweetens with storage. Originated as a pollinated seedling of the French Crabapple. Excellent for eating fresh, cooking and baking. Grown in British Columbia and sparingly in Ontario.

Gravenstein

Available mid-September to December. Medium-to-large fruit, yellowish skin with red striations, creamy flesh, juicy. Excellent for eating fresh, pies and freezing. Good for salads and baking whole. Gravensteins are a popular choice of Nova Scotia orchard growers.

Honeycrisp

Available mid-September to March. Large, round fruit, yellow-green skin with scarlet blush. Cream-coloured flesh, sweet-tart flavour and very crisp. Excellent for eating, good in salads, baking and sauce. Grown in British Columbia, Ontario and Nova Scotia.

Ida Red

Available November to July. Large sweet apple with bright red skin and firm white, juicy flesh. Sweetly tart and spicy. Excellent for pies and baking whole; good for eating fresh, salads, applesauce and freezing. Flavour improves in cold storage. Look for Ida Reds in Ontario and Nova Scotia.

Jonagold

Available mid-September to June. Hybrid of Golden Delicious and Jonathon. Medium-large apple, greenish yellow skin with an orange blush-stripe and crisp yellow flesh. Good for eating fresh, salads, applesauce, pies, baking whole and freezing. Grown mainly in British Columbia and Ontario.

McIntosh

Available late-September to June. Medium-sized apple with red-on-green skin and crisp white, juicy flesh that browns easily. Excellent for eating fresh, good for applesauce and pies but poor for salads, baking whole and freezing. McIntosh apples are grown across Canada.

Northern Spy

Available mid-October to May. Medium-to-large apple with a blush red stripe over green-to-yellow skin and crisp, juicy, aromatic flesh. Excellent for pies and baking whole, good for eating fresh, salads and applesauce. Freezes well. The Northern Spy is grown commercially in Ontario.

Red Delicious

Available late September to August. Medium-to-large heart-shaped apple with a tough, striped or blushed red skin and five distinct bumps on its bottom. An ideal snacking apple, the flesh is greenish-cream, sweet and very juicy. Grown throughout Canada.

Rome Beauty

Available October to May. Large round apple with red striped skin. Flesh is white to pale green, juicy, slightly tart with a mild flavour. Good for fresh eating, cooking and baking. Grown in British Columbia.

Spartan

Available mid-October to May. Hybrid of McIntosh and Yellow Newton. Medium-sized, round, dark-red blushed apple with sweet, crisp, aromatic flesh. Excellent for eating fresh; good for salads, applesauce and pies; poor for baking whole and freezing. Spartans are grown across Canada.

Smoked Breakfast Sausages with Maple Apple Glaze, p.25

Breakfast Fare

No one will question having their "apple a day" when you serve these delightful breakfast treats. From the simple little Okanagan Plum and Apple Crisp to the elegant brunch dish Smoked Breakfast Sausages with Maple Apple Glaze, we are sure you will find something to tempt your palate.

Apple
Butter

The Inn at Spry Point, Spry Point, PE

The chefs at Spry Point suggest that you choose an apple variety that appeals to your personal taste buds, as the end flavour will depend upon the type of apple used. This old-fashioned spicy spread is wonderful with toast, muffins and breads.

3 lb (1.5 kg) apples of choice, peeled, cored and
    quartered
1 cup (250 mL) apple cider
1 ½ cups (375 mL) granulated sugar
½ cup (125 mL) brown sugar
1 ½ tsp (7 mL) ground cinnamon
¼ tsp (1 mL) ground allspice
¼ tsp (1 mL) ground nutmeg
2 tbsp (30 mL) cider vinegar

In a large heavy-bottomed saucepan over medium heat, bring apples and apple cider to a boil. Cover saucepan, reduce heat to simmer and cook, stirring occasionally, until apples are soft, about 25 to 30 minutes (time will vary according to the apple variety).

In a food processor, purée the apples until smooth. Return mixture to the saucepan and add remaining ingredients. Cook over low heat, stirring frequently, until mixture becomes thick, about 30 minutes.

Spoon into plastic containers, cover and freeze, or pour into preserving jars, seal and process in a hot-water bath for 10 minutes.

Makes 5 cups (1.25 L).

Okanagan Plum
and Apple Crisp

Castle on the Mountain Bed & Breakfast,
Vernon, BC

We learned from the owners of this bed and breakfast that a fruit crisp is not just a dessert. This flavourful apple dish will surely start your day off on a sweet note.

1 cup (250 mL) all-purpose flour
½ tsp (2 mL) salt
⅔ cup (150 mL) granulated sugar, portioned
1 tsp (5 mL) ground cinnamon, portioned
½ cup (125 mL) butter
6 medium (4 large) Fuji apples, peeled, cored
   and thinly sliced
3 red plums, pitted and chopped
1 tbsp (15 mL) cornstarch

Preheat oven to 350°F (180°C).

In a medium bowl, combine the flour, salt, ½ cup (125 mL) sugar and ½ tsp (2 mL) cinnamon. Add butter and combine until crumbly. Reserve.

In a large bowl, combine apples and plums with the cornstarch and remaining sugar and cinnamon. Put apple mixture in a lightly greased 2 quart (2 L) baking dish and sprinkle reserved crumb mixture over top. Bake until top is golden and fruit is tender, about 45 to 50 minutes.

Serve warm or chilled.

Serves 6.

The Definitive
Applesauce

The most nutritious and eye-appealing applesauce is one where the apples are cooked unpeeled. The flavour is more intense and the colour is a lovely pink. Adding the sugar and seasoning after the initial cooking also ensures your preferred sweetness level. This sauce makes a great breakfast dish; if you like, sprinkle it with granola for extra zip.

1 ½ lb (750 g) apples, cored and chopped
1 cup (250 mL) water
⅓ cup (75 mL) granulated sugar
2 tsp (10 mL) lemon juice
½ tsp (2 mL) ground cinnamon
pinch of ground nutmeg

Combine apples and water in a saucepan over medium heat. Cover and cook, stirring occasionally, until apples are soft. Remove from heat and press sauce through a strainer to remove peel.

Return applesauce to saucepan; add sugar, lemon, cinnamon and nutmeg and cook, stirring constantly, until the sugar is dissolved. Remove from heat and cool.

Makes 2 ½ cups (625 mL). Recipe is easily doubled.

French Toast
with Sautéed Apples

Gaffer's Gourmet Bistro at Whitehall Country Inn, Clarenville, NL

This combination of mouth-watering ingredients makes a late breakfast or early brunch worth the wait. The chefs at Gaffer's Gourmet Bistro prefer McIntosh apples for their flavour, juiciness and fast cooking.

1 day-old baguette, sliced on an angle, ¼ in (0.5 cm) thick
4 eggs
⅔ cup (150 mL) whole milk (3.25% m.f.)
2 tbsp (30 mL) butter
1 tbsp (15 mL) cinnamon
4 apples, cored, peeled and sliced into ¼-in (0.5-cm) rings
¾ to 1 cup (175 to 250 mL) pure maple syrup
icing sugar for garnish

In a bowl, whisk together eggs and milk until frothy; reserve. In a large skillet over medium heat, melt butter. When butter begins to foam, dip the several slices of bread in the egg mixture and place in the skillet; sprinkle with cinnamon. Fry bread, in batches, until golden brown on both sides, turning once; remove from skillet and reserve in a warm oven.

Place the apple slices in the skillet and sauté, adding more butter if necessary, until lightly browned; turn and sauté the other side until the apples are soft and golden. Pour maple syrup over apples and simmer for 1 minute.

To serve, creatively position the toast on the plates, top with the apples and syrup, and sprinkle with icing sugar.

Serves 6.

Breakfast
Bread Pudding

Cobble House Bed & Breakfast, Cobble Hill, BC

This peaceful haven in the heart of Vancouver Island's wine country serves memorable breakfasts … the type that invite you to linger over yet another cup of coffee. Be sure to treat your family to this breakfast delight!

¼ cup (60 mL) candied ginger, chopped
¼ cup (60 mL) pecan pieces (optional)
¼ cup (60 mL) raisins
¼ cup (60 mL) dried apricots, chopped
1 cup (250 mL) peeled and diced Granny Smith apple
4 slices bread, cubed
1 cup (250 mL) milk
2 eggs, beaten
⅓ cup (75 mL) golden brown sugar
1 tsp (5 mL) ground cinnamon
Custard Cream (recipe follows)
Mint leaves and edible flowers as garnish, optional

Combine ginger, pecans, raisins, apricots, apples and bread cubes in a large bowl. In a separate bowl whisk together milk, eggs, brown sugar and cinnamon. Pour liquid ingredients over dry ingredients and mix to coat. Cover with plastic wrap and refrigerate overnight.

Preheat oven to 400°F (200°C).

Spray 4 individual ramekins with vegetable spray. Divide pudding mixture between ramekins and bake 25 minutes, or until a knife inserted in the center comes out clean.

While puddings are baking prepare Custard Cream and keep warm. To serve, loosen puddings and place baked side up on four serving plates. Carefully spoon custard sauce over puddings and garnish plate with mint leaves and edible flowers.

Serves 4.

Custard Cream (supplied by authors):
½ cup (125 mL) heavy cream (35% m.f.)
½ cup (125 mL) whole milk (3.25% m.f.)
2 egg yolks
2 tbsp (30 mL) icing sugar

Heat, but do not boil, the cream and milk in the top of a double boiler over hot water. Whisk together yolks and icing sugar. Stir a small amount of the hot mixture into the yolks. Return yolks to hot mixture and cook gently, stirring constantly, until mixture lightly coats the back of a spoon. Remove from heat and cover top of sauce with plastic wrap. Keep warm.

Makes 1 cup (250 mL) sauce.

Puffy Apple
Soufflés

Qualicum Bay Bed and Breakfast, Qualicum Beach, BC

Zesty Granny Smith apples are ideal for this dish. We suggest that you not wait for a special occasion to try these breakfast soufflés; they are simple to prepare, and they're a wonderful way to start the day!

4 tbsp (60 mL) butter
2 Granny Smith apples
fresh lemon juice
4 eggs
1 tsp (5 mL) vanilla
¾ cup (175 mL) milk
2 tsp (10 mL) grated lemon zest
¾ cup (175 mL) all-purpose flour
4 tbsp (60 mL) granulated sugar
1tsp (5 mL) ground cinnamon
¼ tsp (1 mL) ground nutmeg
icing sugar, as garnish
pure maple syrup, as garnish

Preheat oven to 425°F (220°C).

Divide butter between four individual 4-in (10-cm) ramekins. Place ramekins in oven until butter bubbles, about 5 minutes.

Peel, core and thinly slice apples. Sprinkle apples with lemon juice and reserve.

In a bowl, beat together eggs, vanilla and milk. Stir in lemon zest and flour and pour into baking dishes, dividing mixture equally. Top with sliced apples and sprinkle with sugar, cinnamon and nutmeg. Bake until puffed, about 20 minutes.

To serve, dust soufflés with icing sugar and drizzle with maple syrup.

Serves 4.

Smoked Breakfast Sausages
with Maple Apple Glaze

A. Hiram Walker Estate Heritage Inn,
St. Andrews, NB

This is an excellent brunch choice, because it
can be prepared in advance and served tableside
in a chafing dish. The innkeeper uses a
combination of Red Delicious and green Granny
Smith apples to provide colour contrast, and
serves the dish accompanied by scrambled eggs
and seasonal fruit.

8 to 12 small pork sausages
⅓ cup (75 mL) butter
¼ cup (60 mL) pecan halves
2 tart apples, cored and sliced
¼ tsp (1 mL) ground cinnamon
generous grating of fresh nutmeg
½ cup (125 mL) pure maple syrup

Pierce sausages with a fork. In a saucepan,
parboil sausages in simmering water for 5
minutes to remove excess fat. Drain saucepan
and reserve sausages.

Heat butter in a large skillet over medium heat;
add pecans, apple slices, cinnamon, nutmeg and
maple syrup and stir to combine. Add sausages;
bring to a simmer and cook, stirring frequently
until apples are barely tender.

Serve with scrambled eggs.

Serves 4.

Savoy Cabbage and Apple Cream Soup, p.31

First Course

Had we suggested to our grandmother that apples could be used in a soup or a salad, she would have scoffed and thought us dotty! If only she could have experienced the smooth Savoy Cabbage and Apple Cream Soup from the San Martello Dining Room at the Dufferin Inn & Suites in Saint John, or British Columbia's West Coast Salmon Salad with Ambrosia Apple Vinaigrette, she would have been a convert to 21st-century cooking.

Salad of Organic Field Greens
with Orange Shallot Vinaigrette

Chives Canadian Bistro, Halifax, NS

To provide contrast, the chef at Chives suggests a mix of mild and bitter salad greens, such as arugula, oak leaf, mâche and radicchio. The salad is topped with a drizzle of vinaigrette bursting with the flavour of shallots.

organic field greens to serve 4
⅔ cup (150 mL) crumbled Danish blue cheese
½ cup (125 mL) smoked almonds
1 Granny Smith apple, cored and cut in julienne
   strips
Orange Shallot Vinaigrette (recipe follows)

Clean greens and arrange on four chilled plates. Sprinkle greens with cheese, smoked almonds and apple strips; drizzle with Orange Shallot Vinaigrette.

Serves 4.

Orange Shallot Vinaigrette:

1 cup (250 mL) freshly squeezed orange juice
zest of one orange, minced
2 small shallots, finely minced
1 tbsp (15 mL) honey vinegar, or 2 tsp (10 mL)
   white vinegar and 1tsp (5 mL) liquid honey
¾ cup (175 mL) light olive oil
salt and pepper
1 tsp (5 mL) sugar (optional)

In a saucepan over medium-high heat, reduce the orange juice to ¼ cup (60 mL). Add zest, shallots and honey vinegar to hot juice. Place mixture in a blender and, with motor running, add olive oil in a slow steady stream until emulsified. Adjust seasoning with salt and pepper; add sugar, if desired; refrigerate.

Makes 1 cup.

Almond Brie with
Apple Chutney

Nemo's Restaurant, Halifax, NS

The chef at Nemo's prepares the almond-encrusted brie in advance and deep-fries it at serving time. We tested the chutney with McIntosh apples and were delighted with the result.

Almond Brie:

8-oz (250-g) round of brie cheese
flour for dusting
egg wash (1 egg beaten with 1 tbsp/15 mL
   water)
½ cup (125 mL) crushed almonds
vegetable oil for frying
Apple Chutney (recipe follows)

Dust brie with flour. Dip in egg wash and roll in crushed almonds, pressing nuts to adhere. Wrap in plastic wrap and refrigerate for several hours.

In a small, deep skillet, heat vegetable oil to a depth of ½ in (1.5 cm). Deep-fry brie in vegetable oil, turning once, until almonds are golden. Be careful not to burn nuts. Carefully remove cheese and drain on paper towels.

Serve with assorted crackers and Apple Chutney.

Serves 4 to 6.

Apple Chutney:

1 ½ cups (375 mL) white vinegar
2 tsp (10 mL) ground coriander
2 tsp (10 mL) ground ginger
2 tsp (10 mL) ground cinnamon
2 tsp (10 mL) dry mustard
2 tsp (10 mL) peppercorns, tied in cheesecloth
3 lb (1.5 kg) apples, peeled, cored and chopped
½ cup (125 mL) raisins
2 cups (500 mL) brown sugar

In a small saucepan, combine vinegar and spices; bring to a boil and cook for one minute.

In a large saucepan combine apples, vinegar mixture, raisins and brown sugar; bring to a boil over medium heat. Lower heat and simmer, stirring occasionally, until fruit is tender and chutney is thick, about 40 minutes.

Remove peppercorns. Pour chutney into sterilized jars and seal.

Makes five to six 8-oz (250-mL) jars.

Savoy Cabbage and
Apple Cream Soup

San Martello Dining Room at Dufferin Inn &
Suites, Saint John, NB

This rich creamy soup from chef and owner
Margret Begner has a wonderful smoky flavour.
The softened apple cubes and curly Savoy
cabbage also give the soup a distinctive texture.
For a lighter soup substitute milk for the cream.

2 cups (500 mL) chicken stock
2 cups (500 mL) Savoy cabbage, julienned in 1-
   in (2.5-cm) lengths
1 cup (250 mL) water
3 cups (750 mL) apple, peeled and cut in small
   cubes
1 tbsp (15 mL) butter
1 large onion, finely chopped
3 slices chicken or turkey bacon, chopped
1 tbsp (15 mL) all-purpose flour
1 cup (250 mL) heavy cream (35% m.f.)
pinch of ground nutmeg
pepper to taste

In a large saucepan over medium heat, bring
chicken stock to a boil. Add cabbage and cook
until slightly softened. Remove cabbage with a
slotted spoon and reserve. Reserve stock in
saucepan.

In another saucepan heat water and add apple
cubes. Cook apple until cubes are just tender.
Remove ¾ cup (175 mL) of the apple cubes with
a slotted spoon and reserve with cabbage.
Continue to cook remaining apples until they
are of a sauce consistency. Remove from heat
and reserve.

Heat butter in a skillet over medium-low heat;
sauté onion and bacon until onion is soft and
bacon is cooked. Drain all but 1 tbsp (15 mL) of
the fat. Add flour to skillet; cook for 1 minute,
stirring constantly.

Whisk onion mixture, applesauce, cream,
nutmeg and pepper into the chicken stock. In a
blender, process soup in batches until creamy.
Return soup to saucepan, add reserved cabbage
and apple cubes and gently reheat, being
careful not to boil. Serve immediately.

Serves 4 to 6.

Caramelized Crispin Apple
under Seared Foie Gras with Watercress and Cardamom Jus

Inn on the Twenty, Jordan, ON

Developed in Japan as Mutsu, this green-with-a-yellow-blush apple was renamed Crispin for North American distribution. Executive chef Kevin Maniaci uses this variety of apple in his appetizer because they hold their shape when cooked.

3 Crispin apples, peeled, cored and thinly sliced
   in rings
½ cup (125 mL) icing sugar
1 tbsp (15 mL) butter
1 tsp (5 mL) cardamom seeds, toasted*
¼ cup (60 mL) Madeira
⅓ cup veal jus or demi-glace
juice of 1 lemon
salt and freshly ground pepper, to taste
6 oz (170 g) foie gras
freshly grated nutmeg
4 oz (125 g) watercress or any peppery green

Lightly dust apple slices with icing sugar and sauté in butter over medium heat for 20 to 30 seconds on each side. Remove apples from pan and cool on a plate lined with waxed paper. Once cool, arrange slices in four neat towers or piles on a baking sheet lined with parchment paper.

Place apples in a preheated 350°F (180°C) oven for 6 to 8 minutes or until the edges of the apple towers begin to crisp. Remove from oven and keep warm.

Gently toast cardamom seeds in a saucepan over medium heat for 2 minutes, shaking pan occasionally. Deglaze pan with Madeira and simmer until the volume of liquid in the pot reduces to 1 tbsp (15 mL).

Stir in veal stock or demi-glace and bring to a boil. Season with salt, pepper and lemon juice. Strain sauce to remove seeds. Keep warm.

Lightly score the surface of the duck liver in a criss-cross fashion and season with salt, pepper and freshly ground nutmeg. Place liver in a pre-heated heavy-bottomed frying pan over high heat, scored side down. Once liver has been in the pan 30 seconds, flip with a spatula and turn off heat. Leave the duck liver in the pan for another 30 seconds, and then remove to a clean kitchen towel to absorb any extra fat. Cut liver into four equal portions.

To serve, place a crisped apple tower on an appetizer plate. Place a small amount of watercress on top of the apple. Position a duck liver portion on top of the cress; drizzle with about 1 tsp (5 mL) cardamom jus. Garnish plate with additional watercress and a few drops of cardamom jus.

Serves 4.

*Cardamom is sold in small pods about the size of a cranberry. Each pod contains about 20 tiny seeds. Remove the seeds by cutting open the pod and scraping out the seeds.

Apple Butternut
Squash Soup

Deerhurst Resort, Huntsville, ON

Executive chef Rory Golden notes that the apples and maple syrup combine in this soup to make a subtle sweetness that he offsets with the juice of a fresh lime.

2 tbsp (30 mL) butter
3 cups (750 mL) cubed butternut squash
1 cup (250 mL) finely diced onion
2 McIntosh apples, peeled, cored and cubed
½ cup (125 mL) apple juice
4 cups (1 L) chicken stock
¼ cup (60 mL) pure maple syrup
½ cup (125 mL) heavy cream (35% m.f.)
juice of ½ fresh lime
salt and pepper, to taste

Heat butter in a heavy-bottomed saucepan over medium-high heat; add squash, onions and apples and sauté until onions are transparent and squash is slightly softened, about 10 minutes. Add apple juice and reduce liquid by one-half. Add stock and maple syrup and reduce heat to medium-low. Cover and simmer, stirring occasionally, until squash is tender, about 30 minutes. Cool slightly.

In a blender, purée soup in batches until smooth. Return soup to saucepan and bring to a simmer. Heat cream in a separate saucepan and slowly whisk into soup. Season with salt, pepper and lime juice.

Serves 4 to 6.

West Coast Salmon Salad
with Ambrosia Apple Vinaigrette

Sequoia Grill at the Teahouse, Vancouver, BC

Ambrosia apples ripen in the autumn and are in season for three short weeks. These delightful apples have a distinct honeyed and slightly perfumed flavour. The flesh is tender and juicy, with a very fine, crisp texture.

1 lb (500 g) salmon, cut in 4 pieces
½ cup (125 mL) tamari sauce
½ cup (125 mL) brown sugar
1 tsp (5 mL) dried chilies
dash salt and pepper
4 hearts of romaine, torn into bite-sized pieces
2 avocados, halved
16 cherry tomatoes, halved
2 pink grapefruits, peeled, pith removed and
    segmented
4 hard-boiled eggs, sliced
10 strips bacon, fried crisp and crumbled, for
    garnish (optional)
Ambrosia Apple Vinaigrette (recipe follows)

Rinse salmon and pat dry. In a shallow glass dish combine tamari sauce, brown sugar, dried chilies, salt and pepper. Marinate salmon, refrigerated, for 30 minutes; drain.

Preheat oven to 350°F (180°C).

Arrange drained salmon on a non-stick roasting pan and bake until cooked, about 8 to 10 minutes. Set aside.

Divide romaine between four salad plates. Decoratively arrange avocado slices, cherry tomatoes, grapefruit segments and hard-boiled egg slices over lettuce. Top with warm salmon and garnish, if desired, with a sprinkling of bacon. Drizzle Ambrosia Apple Vinaigrette over salads.

Serves 4.

Ambrosia Apple Vinaigrette:
1 Ambrosia apple, peeled, cored and sliced
2 tsp (10 mL) minced shallots
4 fresh basil leaves
1 tsp (5 mL) minced ginger root
3 tbsp (45 mL) apple cider vinegar
3 tbsp (45 mL) mirin
1 ½ tbsp (22 mL) tamari sauce
1 cup (250 mL) canola oil
salt and pepper to taste

Place apple, shallot, basil leaves, ginger root, vinegar, mirin and tamari in a blender and process until smooth. With motor running, add oil in a slow steady stream, processing until emulsified. Season to taste with salt and pepper.

Makes 1 ½ cups (375 mL).

Baby Spinach Salad
with Pancetta Bacon, Brie and Green Apple Vinaigrette

Westover Inn, St. Marys, ON

The juice reduction of the vinaigrette provides an intense aromatic flavour which is highly complementary to the pancetta and creamy cheese in this spinach salad.

6 slices pancetta*
fresh baby spinach salad greens to serve 6
Green Apple Vinaigrette (recipe follows)
6 wedges Sir Laurier D'Arethabaska cheese (or other soft brie-style cheese)

On a baking sheet, broil pancetta under broiler until golden, being careful not to burn. Remove from oven and reserve.

Arrange salad greens on serving plates, drizzle with vinaigrette, top with pancetta and serve with wedge of cheese.

Makes 6 servings.

Green Apple Vinaigrette:
2 cups (500 mL) organic apple juice or cider
1 ½ tbsp (22 mL) lemon juice
1 tsp (5 mL) lemon zest
¾ cup (175 mL) vegetable oil
salt and pepper

In a saucepan over medium-high heat, reduce apple juice to ⅓ cup (75 mL). Cool slightly.

In a blender, combine reduced juice, lemon juice and zest; blend on high for 30 seconds. With blender running, add the vegetable oil in a slow steady stream until emulsified.

Makes 1 ¼ cups (300 mL).

*Pancetta (cured Italian bacon) is available in the deli section of most supermarkets or Italian grocery stores.

Apple, Celery
and Blue Cheese Soup

Keltic Lodge, Ingonish Beach, NS

Dale Nichols, executive chef at Keltic Lodge, has created a bisque-style soup with perfect flavour balance. You will find the soup subtle, smooth and creamy — a perfect first course to an elegant meal. We prepared this soup twice, once using heavy cream and the second time using blend (12% m.f.). While the heavy cream created a full-bodied soup, the flavour was not compromised in the lighter version.

⅓ cup (75 mL) butter
¾ large white onion, finely diced
3 cloves garlic, minced
5 stalks celery, chopped
3 large juicy apples, cored, peeled and diced
3 tbsp (45 mL) all-purpose flour
6 cups (1.5 L) vegetable stock (or chicken stock)
6 oz (185 g) blue cheese
¾ cup (175 mL) heavy cream (35% m.f.)
salt and white pepper

Melt butter in a heavy saucepan over medium heat. Add onion and garlic and sauté until softened, about 3 to 5 minutes. Add celery and sauté until soft, about 3 minutes. Add apples and sauté 3 minutes.

Sprinkle flour over mixture; stir and cook for 1 minute. Slowly add stock, stirring constantly to avoid lumps. Bring to a boil; reduce to simmer and cook, loosely covered, until all is soft. Add the blue cheese and stir until melted. Add the cream, cover, and simmer on low heat for 5 minutes.

In a blender, purée soup in batches until smooth and creamy. Return soup to saucepan, adjust seasoning with salt and white pepper, and gently reheat.

Serves 6.

Mixed Greens with Roasted
Garlic, Apple and Maple Vinaigrette

Ste. Anne's Country Inn & Spa, Grafton, ON

In this recipe, executive chef Christopher Ennew uses roasted garlic to flavour his salad dressing. Do not be afraid to use half a roasted garlic bulb. Unlike chopping or crushing raw garlic cloves to release their essential oils and provide a sharp flavour, roasting garlic mellows and sweetens the garlic flavour.

1 firm apple, peeled, cored and sliced
pinch ground nutmeg
pinch ground cinnamon
1 tsp (5 mL) pure maple syrup
½ whole garlic bulb, roasted*
2 tbsp (30 mL) maple or white vinegar
2 tbsp (30 mL) apple juice
½ cup (125 mL) vegetable oil
¼ cup (60 mL) olive oil
salt and pepper
assorted salad greens to serve 6 to 8

Preheat oven to 375°F (190°C).

Toss prepared apple slices with nutmeg, cinnamon and maple syrup. Place on a pie plate and bake in oven for 10 minutes. Reserve.

Place apples in a food processor. Squeeze roasted garlic out of skins and add to apples. Pulse to combine; add vinegar and apple juice. Mix well, scrape down sides with a spatula and mix again. With motor running slowly, add oils in a slow steady stream and process until emulsified. Adjust seasoning with salt and pepper.

Store refrigerated in a tightly covered container for up to 1 week. Shake before serving.

Makes 1 cup (250 mL).

To serve: arrange salad greens on serving plates and drizzle with vinaigrette.

Serves 6 to 8.

*To roast a garlic bulb:
Slice the top off a whole head of garlic, cutting through the cloves. Place cut side up in a baking dish, brush with olive oil and roast at 350°F (180°C) until golden brown and soft to the touch, about 50 minutes.

Fennel-seared Scallops with Apple and Celeriac Purée, p.42

Main Course

We suggest that you try some of these tantalizing dishes and take the apple into an entirely new dimension. Rack of Lamb with Apple Demi-glace from the Dunes of Prince Edward Island or Apple and Tarragon Stuffed Pork Roast from Winnipeg's Inn at the Forks are but two examples of creative Canadian cooking.

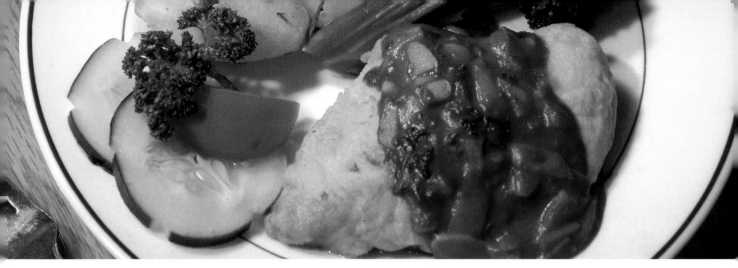

Chicken Normandy
with Apple Demi-glace

Nemo's Restaurant, Halifax, NS

At Nemo's they serve these tender breasts of chicken napped with apple demi-glace, surrounded by roasted potatoes and steamed seasonal vegetables. We are sure you will find the recipe easy to follow and that you will be delighted with the results.

4 boneless chicken breasts, 6 oz (180 g) each
¼ cup (60 mL) all-purpose flour
dash salt and pepper
1 tsp (5 mL) chopped fresh thyme leaves
   (¼ tsp/1 mL dried)
2 tbsp (30 mL) vegetable oil
Apple Demi-glace (recipe follows)
Apple Chutney, for garnish (see recipe on page 28)

Preheat oven to 375°F (190°C).

Rinse chicken breasts and pat dry. In a bowl, combine flour, salt, pepper and thyme. Dredge chicken in flour mixture, coating lightly.

Heat oil over high heat in a heavy ovenproof skillet; quickly brown chicken, turning once. Place skillet in oven and bake for 5 to 7 minutes, or until chicken is no longer pink in the centre.

Serve chicken napped with warm apple demi-glace and chutney on the side.

Serves 4.

Apple Demi-glace:
8 tsp (40 mL) demi-glace powder (available in
   most grocery stores)
⅔ cup (150 mL) cold water
2 ½ tbsp (37 mL) red wine
dash of Worcestershire sauce
¼ cup (60 mL) finely diced onion
6 tbsp (90 mL) Apple Chutney (see recipe page
   28)
2 to 3 tbsp (30 to 45 mL) heavy cream (35%
   m.f.)

In a small saucepan over medium heat, combine all ingredients; bring to a boil, stirring constantly. Reduce heat and simmer until slightly thickened. Set aside and keep warm.

Anatra
Melata

Quattro on Fourth, Vancouver, BC

Granny Smith apples are a popular West Coast choice for either cooking or eating. Executive chef Bradford Ellis combines this firm green apple with maple syrup and brandy to sauce his duck breasts. He suggests serving the dish with a hearty accompaniment such as polenta or roasted potatoes.

4 Muscovy duck breasts, 6 oz (170 g) each
¼ cup (60 mL) brandy
½ cup (125 mL) pure maple syrup
1 Granny Smith apple, cored and sliced
1 cup (250 mL) chicken stock
salt and freshly ground black pepper
¼ cup (60 mL) sliced almonds, toasted*

Preheat oven to 350°F (160°C).

Score skin side of duck and place, skin side down, in a dry ovenproof skillet over medium heat. Cook duck until skin is crispy and golden. Turn breasts over and place skillet in oven. Roast for 10 minutes or until internal temperature reaches 165°F (75°C). Tent with foil and reserve.

Deglaze skillet over medium-high heat with brandy and maple syrup. Add sliced apple and chicken stock. Reduce to sauce consistency, about 10 to 12 minutes. Season to taste with salt and black pepper.

To serve: slice duck breast and fan out on a plate. Spoon sauce over duck and sprinkle with toasted almonds.

Serves 4.

*To toast almonds:
Spread nuts on a baking sheet and bake in a preheated 325°F (160°C) oven, stirring or shaking the pan often, about 5 to 7 minutes or until golden and fragrant. Let cool.

Fennel-seared Scallops
with Apple and Celeriac Purée

Oban Inn, Niagara-on-the-Lake, ON

This seafood entrée, created by Andy Hall, sous chef at Oban Inn, has great visual appeal and will delight your palate with its contrasting textures and flavours.

1 tbsp (15 mL) butter
1 shallot, thinly sliced
3 Granny Smith or Crispin apples, peeled, cored and cut in ¼-in (0.5-cm) dice
2 lb (1 kg) celeriac (celery root), peeled and cut in ¼-in (0.5-cm) dice
salt and pepper
1 ½ cups (375 mL) apple cider
3 tbsp (45 mL) apple cider vinegar
¼ cup (60 mL) unsalted butter
1 ½ tbsp (22 mL) fennel seed, portioned
½ tbsp (7 mL) coarse sea salt
1 tsp (5 mL) pepper
1 ½ lbs (750 g) large scallops
2 tsp (10 mL) olive oil
12 sage leaves, fresh or fried*

In a large heavy-bottomed saucepan, melt butter over low heat. Add shallot, apples and celeriac; cover and sweat until vegetables are softened. The time this takes will depend on the texture of the celeriac and may be about 1 hour or longer. In a food processor, purée mixture until smooth. Season with salt and pepper. Reserve, keep warm.

In a small, deep saucepan combine cider and vinegar; bring to a vigorous boil and reduce by three-quarters. Remove from heat and whisk in butter to form a butter sauce. Reserve and keep warm.

In a small bowl, combine 1 tbsp (15 mL) fennel seeds and salt. In another bowl, combine remaining fennel seeds and pepper.

Wash scallops and pat dry. Dip one side of scallops into fennel seed and salt mixture and press to adhere; dip other side into fennel seed and pepper mixture.

Heat olive oil in a heavy skillet over medium-high heat; add scallops, fennel-and-salt-side down, and sear until golden and partially cooked. Flip and cook until desired doneness, being careful not to over cook.

To serve: portion celeriac purée on centre of plates, place scallops on top and drizzle cider butter sauce around. Garnish with fresh or fried sage leaves.

Serves 4.

*To fry sage leaves:
Heat 2 tbsp (30 mL) vegetable oil in a small
skillet over medium-high heat. Add sage leaves
and quickly crisp, being careful to avoid oil
splattering. Remove leaves and dry on paper
towel to absorb excess oil.

Apple and Tarragon
Stuffed Pork Roast with
Whole Mustard Port Wine Sauce

Current Restaurant at Inn at the Forks,
Winnipeg, MB

Barry Saunters, executive chef at the Current Restaurant, frequently prepares this popular dish for their Sunday brunch buffet. He feels that the combination of apple and tarragon are a perfect match, much like tomato and basil or rosemary and garlic. Chef Saunters usually makes the sauce as a 'jus.' If you prefer a creamy style gravy simply combine all-purpose flour and softened butter, shape into small balls and whisk them into the sauce until it reaches the desired consistency.

1 boneless centre-cut pork loin roast, 3 to 4 lb
  (1.75 to 2 kg)
1 tbsp (15 mL) vegetable oil
sea salt and coarsely ground black pepper

Stuffing:
1 tbsp (15 mL) vegetable oil
1 shallot, peeled and finely diced
1 large Granny Smith apple, cored and finely diced
½ oz (15 g) fresh tarragon, roughly chopped
sea salt and black pepper

Sauce:
2 cups (500 mL) beef stock
1 tsp (5 mL) vegetable oil
1 shallot, peeled and finely diced
1 ½ cups (375 mL) port wine
¾ cup (175 mL) heavy cream (35% m.f.)
1 ½ tbsp (22 mL) grainy mustard
salt and pepper

Prepare the stuffing: heat vegetable oil in a skillet over medium heat; add shallots and sauté until softened, being careful not to brown. Add apples and cook for 2 to 3 minutes until they are cooked but still firm. Add tarragon and season with salt and pepper to taste. Remove from heat and cool.

Preheat oven to 375°F (190°C).

Using a long narrow knife, make a hole that runs lengthwise through the centre of the loin. Turn the knife 90 degrees and insert again, creating an X. Open up the cut with your fingers, to create a 1 ½ in (3.75 cm) wide opening to hold the stuffing.

Working from both ends, stuff the apple mixture into the pork loin. When filled, if necessary, secure the roast with butcher's twine. Season the outside with sea salt and a generous amount of freshly ground black pepper.

Heat vegetable oil in a heavy skillet over medium-high heat. Brown pork on all sides, about 8 minutes total. Transfer loin to a roasting pan and bake until thermometer inserted into the meat reaches 160°F (70°C); make sure the thermometer is not pushed into the stuffing. Transfer to a cutting board, tent with foil and let stand 15 minutes.

Prepare the sauce: heat the skillet used for searing the roast on medium-high heat. When hot, add the beef stock and deglaze, stirring constantly. Strain through a fine mesh sieve into a bowl, and reserve.

Heat remaining 1 tsp (5 mL) oil in a saucepan; add remaining shallots and sauté until translucent. Add port wine and boil until reduced by one-quarter. Add beef stock and reduce by one-half. Add cream and simmer for 3 to 5 minutes. Stir in mustard and season to taste with salt and pepper.

To serve: slice pork loin in ½-in (1-cm) rounds and top with sauce.

Serves 6 to 8.

Rack of Lamb
with Apple Demi-glace

The Dunes Café and Gardens, Brackley Beach, PE

With commercial demi-glace mix, available in most grocery stores, this is a quick and delicious entrée, especially if you make the sauce in advance. All of the dishes prepared at the Dunes Café and Gardens are served in decorative pottery made on the premises.

2 racks of lamb, 12 to 14 oz (375 to 400 g) each
2 tbsp (30 mL) vegetable oil
1 ½ oz (34 g) package demi-glace mix
1 ¼ cups (310 mL) water
2 tbsp (30 mL) red wine
1 small bay leaf
1 sprig fresh rosemary
2 apples, peeled, cored and sliced
1 ½ tbsp (22 mL) raisins, optional
salt and pepper

Preheat oven to 375°F (190°C).

In an ovenproof skillet heat oil over medium-high heat; briefly sear lamb racks on both sides. Remove to oven and bake for 25 to 30 minutes for rare, or until desired, doneness. Remove from oven and let stand for 5 minutes.

Prepare sauce while lamb is baking. In a small saucepan, whisk demi-glace mix into water and bring to simmer. Add wine, bay leaf and rosemary, bring back to simmer and cook 3 minutes. Discard bay leaf and rosemary and add prepared apples and raisins. Bring back to simmer and cook 5 minutes, adding additional wine if the sauce becomes too thick. Season with salt and pepper and reserve, keeping warm.

To serve: Slice lamb between the bones. Pour sauce in centre of warmed plates and arrange 3 to 4 ribs per serving on pool of sauce. Serve with vegetables of choice.

Serves 4.

Pickerel with Maple,
Butternut Squash and Apple Cider Glaze

Deerhurst Resort, Huntsville, ON

Ontarians are generally referring to walleye, a member of the perch family, when they speak of pickerel. True pickerel are members of the pike family of which there are three varieties native to Canada — the redfin, grass and chain. Whether you select pickerel, walleye or another white-fleshed fish like perch or tilapia, you will enjoy the subtle sweetness the cider, maple and apple bring to this main-course creation from Rory Golden, chef at Deerhurst Resort.

2 tbsp (30 mL) vegetable oil
3 tbsp (45 mL) butter, portioned
1 ½ lbs (750 g) pickerel fillets
salt and white pepper
¼ cup (60 mL) all-purpose flour
½ cup (125 mL) butternut squash, cut in ¼-in (0.5-cm) dice
½ McIntosh apple, peeled and cut in ¼-in (0.5-cm) dice
½ cup (125 mL) apple cider
2 tbsp (30 mL) pure maple syrup
fresh lemon juice to taste

Preheat oven to 350°F (180°C).

Preheat an ovenproof skillet over medium-high heat and add oil and 1 tbsp (15 mL) butter. While skillet is heating, season fillets with salt and white pepper and dredge in flour. Place fillets in skillet, skin side up, and brown for 2 to 3 minutes. Turn fillets over and transfer skillet to oven. Bake 6 to 8 minutes or until fish is just cooked through. Remove fillets from pan and keep warm.

Return skillet to stove over medium-high heat. Add 1 tbsp (15 mL) butter and diced squash, sauté for 2 to 3 minutes. Add apple and sauté for 1 minute. Add apple cider and let liquid reduce by half, about 3 to 4 minutes. Add maple syrup and remaining 1 tbsp (15 mL) butter and quickly bring to a boil. Adjust seasoning with lemon juice to taste.

To serve: pour glaze over fillets and serve immediately.

Serves 4.

Sautéed Scallops
on Green Apple Risotto

Wellington Court Restaurant, St. Catharines, ON

You will find the green apple risotto a pleasing complement to the succulent scallops in this creation from Erik Peacock, executive chef at Wellington Court. While the risotto's mild flavour does not overpower the sweet and delicate seafood, it does provide a contrast with its *al dente* texture.

4 to 5 cups (1 to 1.25 L) chicken stock
¼ cup (60 mL) extra virgin olive oil, portioned
3 tbsp (45 mL) chopped shallot
1 ½ cups (375 mL) Arborio rice
1 cup (250 mL) Granny Smith apple peeled, cored and diced
½ cup (125 mL) dry white wine
3 tbsp (45 mL) unsalted butter
salt and pepper
1 ½ lbs (750 g) large scallops
2 thin slices proscuitto ham, diced

In a saucepan, heat chicken stock until hot but not simmering; cover and keep at this temperature.

In a heavy saucepan, heat 2 tbsp (30 mL) olive oil over low heat; add shallots, cover and cook for 2 minutes, until softened. Add rice and cook, stirring constantly, until grains are slightly transparent. Pour in wine; cook, stirring often, and then add stock, ½ cup (125 mL) at a time, allowing rice to completely absorb liquid each time. Stir in the apple about 10 minutes into this process. Continue to add stock and cook until rice is *al dente* (firm to the bite), about 25 minutes.

Remove from heat, stir in butter and season with salt and pepper to taste. Reserve and keep warm.

Wash scallops and pat dry. Heat a heavy-bottomed skillet to medium-high and add remaining olive oil. Add scallops and sauté until browned but just barely cooked, about 3 to 5 minutes.

To serve: portion risotto on serving plates, place scallops and their cooking liquid on the risotto, and sprinkle with proscuitto.

Serves 4.

Grilled Ontario Pork
Tenderloin with Riesling Cream Corn and Asparagus Crispin Apple Fritters

Hillebrand Estates Winery Restaurant, Niagara-on-the-Lake, ON

Executive chef Tony de Luca creates a beautiful dish by combining colourful and fresh Riesling Cream Corn and apple. The fritters are a beautiful combination with the pork tenderloin.

2 pork tenderloins, 1 lb (450 g) each
2 tbsp (30 mL) olive oil
salt, pepper and cayenne pepper
Riesling Cream Corn (recipe follows)
Asparagus Crispin Apple Fritters (recipe follows)

Brush pork with oil. Season with salt, pepper and cayenne to taste. On a grill over high heat, cook tenderloins for 8 minutes; turn and grill for about 4 minutes longer or until just a hint of pink remains inside. Cut into 1 ½-in (4-cm) slices.

Spoon about ¼ cup (60 mL) of the Riesling Cream Corn onto each of 4 warmed plates. Fan 3 slices of pork tenderloin on top of sauce. Arrange 3 fritters attractively around pork.

Serves 4.

Chef's tip: The fritter mixture can be made up to 2 hours in advance.

Asparagus Crispin Apple Fritters:
¾ cup (175 mL) all-purpose flour
½ cup (125 mL) bread flour
3 tsp (15 mL) baking powder
1 tsp (5 mL) salt
2 large eggs, beaten
2 cups (500 mL) milk
2 tbsp (30 mL) maple syrup
¾ cup (175 mL) chopped pecans
½ Crispin apple, peeled, cored and chopped into
   ¼-in (0.5-cm) pieces
3 tsp (15 mL) minced fresh ginger root
½ cup (125 mL) peeled asparagus, chopped in
   ½-in (1-cm) pieces
3 cups (750 mL) vegetable oil

In a large bowl, combine all-purpose and bread flours, baking powder and salt.

In a separate bowl, blend together eggs, milk and maple syrup. Stir in pecans, apple, ginger and asparagus.

Stir apple mixture into flour mixture until blended.

In a deep saucepan, heat oil over high heat to 350°F (180°C); spoon a heaping tablespoon of batter into hot oil and cook until golden brown. Remove with a slotted spoon and let drain on paper towel. Repeat with remaining batter. Keep warm.

Riesling Cream Corn:
6 ears corn
1 tbsp (15 mL) olive oil
1 shallot, finely diced
1 clove garlic, minced
½ sweet red pepper, cut into ¼-in
   (0.5-cm) pieces
½ sweet yellow pepper, cut into ¼-in
   (0.5-cm) pieces
¼ cup (60 mL) riesling or other white wine
½ cup (125 mL) heavy cream (35% m.f.)
salt and pepper

Husk and clean corn. Slice off kernels.
In a skillet, heat oil over medium-high heat; sauté shallots, garlic, corn and red and yellow peppers for 2 minutes. Add wine and reduce to 1 tbsp (15 mL). Blend in cream; add salt and pepper to taste. Keep warm.

Apple Ricotta Lasagna
with Béchamel and Fresh Herbs

Wellington Court Restaurant, St. Catharines, ON

For a new take on an old classic, executive chef Erik Peacock notes that he often serves this dish in the autumn. While it makes a delicious vegetarian main course, Chef Peacock comments that he often pairs it with a double-cut chop of wild boar.

16 lasagna noodles
4 lbs (2 kg) Crispin or other firm cooking apples
4 large cloves garlic, minced
1 ½ tbsp (22 mL) olive oil
salt and pepper
16 oz (450 g) ricotta
1 large egg
3 tbsp (45 mL) fresh herbs, roughly chopped
   (thyme, tarragon, chives, etc)
Béchamel Sauce (recipe follows)

Cook lasagna noodles according to package directions for *al dente*; drain and rinse with cold water to stop cooking process. Drain again and spread in a single layer on tea towels to dry.

Peel, core and slice apples into wedges. Place apples and garlic in a large bowl, drizzle with olive oil and sprinkle with salt and pepper; toss to coat. Heat a large skillet over medium-high heat and sauté apple slices, in batches, until just wilted and both sides are lightly browned.

Remove to a platter and set aside.

In a medium bowl whisk together the ricotta and egg. Set aside.

Prepare béchamel sauce and set aside.

To assemble, lightly grease a 9 x 12-in (23 x 31-cm) lasagna pan with olive oil. Spread a small amount of béchamel sauce over the bottom and top with a layer of noodles. Then layer one-third of the apple slices, one-third of the ricotta mixture and one-third of the béchamel sauce. Sprinkle with 1 tbsp (15 mL) fresh herbs and top with another layer of noodles. Press down lightly. Repeat two times to make 3 layers in all, ending with sauce.

Cover tightly with foil and bake in a 325°F (160°C) oven until hot and bubbly, about 1 hour. Remove the foil and continue to bake until lightly browned. Remove from oven and let set about 15 minutes before serving.

Serves 6 to 8.

Béchamel Sauce:

6 tbsp (90 mL) olive oil

6 tbsp (90 mL) all-purpose flour

1 cup (250 mL) dry white wine

1 cup (250 mL) milk

1 cup (250 mL) coffee cream (18% m.f.)

salt and pepper to taste

⅛ tsp (0.5 mL) freshly grated nutmeg

½ cup (125 mL) freshly grated Parmesan cheese

In a saucepan over medium heat, stir oil and flour to combine. Cook, stirring constantly, for about 2 minutes, being careful not to allow the roux to darken. Gradually add the wine, milk and cream, about ½ cup (125 mL) at a time, whisking vigorously to incorporate. Cook over medium-low heat, stirring often, until thickened and just starting to boil, about 10 minutes.

Remove from heat, season with salt, pepper, nutmeg and Parmesan cheese. Whisk until cheese is incorporated. Cool slightly.

Makes 3 cups (750mL).

Hot Mulled Cider, p.58

Accompaniments

Chefs create side dishes to highlight and complement, but never overpower, their featured entrée. They realize that well-chosen accompaniments can turn an ordinary meal into a memorable dining occasion. In this section, we have selected a variety of apple-based accompaniments for you to prepare in your own kitchen.

Baked Apple
Accompaniment

Gowrie House Country Inn, Sydney Mines, NS

Autumn brings a new crop of tangy apples and
at Gowrie House, the chef features this dish
with pork and chicken entrées.

2 or 3 baking apples (Cortland, McIntosh, Spy)
½ cup (125 mL) granulated sugar
½ tsp (2 mL) ground allspice
2 tbsp (30 mL) melted butter

Preheat oven to 350°F (180°C).

Peel, core and section apples into eighths.
Combine sugar and allspice and coat the apple
segments. Place apples in a shallow baking dish
and drizzle with melted butter. Bake for 25 to
30 minutes until soft and bubbly.

Serves 4 to 6.

Hot Mulled
Cider

We are providing two versions of hot mulled cider. One "with" and one "without." Pick your potion!

Mulled Cider Without!!

1 qt (1 L) sweet apple cider
1 tsp (5 mL) whole cloves
1 tsp (5 mL) whole allspice
2-in (5-cm) piece of cinnamon stick

Combine ingredients in a large saucepan or coffee urn and heat slowly for half an hour. *Do not boil.* Discard spices and if desired, strain. Serve piping hot.

Yields 6 servings.

Mulled Cider With!!

1 qt (1 L) sweet apple cider
¼ cup (60 mL) dark rum
3 tbsp (45 mL) brown sugar
2 tbsp (30 mL) lemon juice
2-in (5-cm) piece cinnamon stick
¼ tsp (1 mL) whole allspice

Combine all ingredients in a large saucepan and heat until nearly bubbling. *Do not boil.*

Strain into six serving cups.

Braised Red Cabbage
with Apples and Onion

Duncreigan Country Inn, Mabou, NS

Colourful in its presentation, this braised cabbage dish is an excellent accompaniment to roasted pork or turkey.

1 large onion, thinly sliced
1 tbsp (15 mL) vegetable oil
1 small red cabbage, cored and very thinly sliced
½ cup (125 mL) chicken broth
2 tsp (10 mL) balsamic vinegar
2 firm red cooking apples, peeled, cored and cut into wedges
2 tbsp (30 mL) cream sherry
¼ cup (60 mL) pure maple syrup

Over low heat, sauté sliced onion in oil, stirring frequently, until caramelized. This procedure takes about 30 minutes. Reserve onion.

Over low heat, simmer thinly sliced cabbage in chicken broth and vinegar until cabbage is tender, about 45 to 50 minutes, stirring occasionally. Spread onions over cabbage and top with apple wedges. Drizzle with sherry and maple syrup and continue to cook, covered, for 15 minutes.

To serve, carefully ladle with a slotted spoon onto plates, trying not to disturb the layers.

Serves 4 to 6.

Apple Cranberry
Compote

River Café Island Park, Calgary, AB

Chefs at River Café Island Park frequently feature game such as wild boar on their menu. They have found that this slightly tart compote complements the boar as well as other pork dishes.

1 tbsp (15 mL) shallots, minced
1 tsp (5 mL) fresh ginger, minced
1 tsp (5 mL) vegetable oil
1 tbsp (15 mL) granulated sugar
2 tbsp (30 mL) sherry vinegar
1 tbsp (15 mL) fresh lemon juice
¼ cup (60 mL) apple juice
2 apples, peeled and cut in ½-in (1-cm) dice
½ cup (125 mL) dried cranberries
pinch each mustard seeds, ground nutmeg and
    ground cinnamon

Heat oil in a saucepan over low heat; add shallots and ginger and sweat until softened. Add sugar, vinegar, lemon juice and apple juice. Raise heat and bring to a boil. Add remaining ingredients, reduce heat to simmer and continue to cook until almost all of the liquid is absorbed and the apple is tender.

Makes 1 ¼ cups (310 mL) sauce.

Apple and Rutabaga
Casserole

Blomidon Inn, Wolfville, NS

Donna Laceby from Blomidon Inn shared this recipe with us a number of years ago. It is a great accompaniment for all roasted meat entrées and has become a family favourite at our homes.

Please note that what some Canadians call turnips are in fact rutabagas. While rutabagas and turnips are from the same family, rutabagas are large with yellowish flesh and turnips are smaller and have white flesh. They are interchangeable in this recipe.

1 large rutabaga, 2 ½ to 3 lb (1.25 to 1.5 kg), cooked and mashed
1 tsp (5 mL) granulated sugar
1 cup (250 mL) water
2 tart apples, cored and sliced
¼ cup (60 mL) heavy cream (35% m.f.)
2 tbsp (30 mL) butter

Preheat oven to 350°F (180°C).

Prepare turnip and reserve. In a skillet heat sugar and water and poach apple slices until barely soft. Remove apples with a slotted spoon.

Layer mashed turnip and apples in a small casserole. Top with cream and dot with butter. Bake for 30 minutes.

Serves 4 to 6.

Apple Tomato
Chutney

Liscombe Lodge, Liscomb, NS

This recipe was shared by the chef at Liscombe Lodge on Nova Scotia's Eastern Shore. The chutney's pungent flavour and wonderful colour make it a fitting addition to meat and seafood entrées.

3 lb (1.5 kg) tomatoes
4 cups (1 L) apples, peeled, cored and diced
1 cup (250 mL) seedless raisins
½ cup (125 mL) finely chopped onion
1 cup (250 mL) brown sugar, firmly packed
½ cup (125 mL) maple syrup
⅔ cup (150 mL) cider vinegar
1 ½ tsp (7 mL) mixed pickling spices
½ tsp (2 mL) whole cloves

Bring a saucepan of water to a boil, immerse tomatoes until skin begins to soften (depending on ripeness of fruit, this may only be a few seconds). Remove with a slotted spoon and immediately slide off the skin. Cut away stem section and dice.

Place tomatoes in a bowl, cover and put a heavy weight on top. Press overnight and in the morning pour off the juice.

Transfer tomatoes to a large saucepan and add apples, raisins, onion, sugar, maple syrup and vinegar. Tie up spices in a cheesecloth bag and add to the saucepan. Bring to a boil, stirring constantly. Reduce heat and simmer until thick, about 1 ½ hours, stirring occasionally. Remove spice bag. Pour chutney into hot sterilized jars and seal.

Makes six 8-oz (250-mL) jars.

Roasted Apple and Rosemary Tart, p.72

Sweet Endings

May we present an offering of apple desserts that we promise are as good as Mom's apple pie? Be sure to try the sophisticated Torta Di Mele Alla Panna from La Perla Restaurant or Blomidon Inn's award-winning Baked Apple Dessert.

Caramelized Apple
Upside-down Cake

Bishop's Restaurant, Vancouver, BC

This is the perfect dessert for a cold winter night. The caramelized apples are moist and the spicy ginger cake creates a beautiful topping when the cake is inverted. The chef suggests the best apples to use are Fuji, Gala or Spartan. This cake is best served warm, fresh from the oven, with either a little whipped cream or vanilla ice cream as garnish.

butter for greasing
all-purpose flour for dusting
2 tbsp (30 mL) butter, melted
¾ cup (175 mL) brown sugar, portioned
¾ cup (175 mL) water
½ cup (125 mL) molasses
1 tsp (5 mL) baking soda
2 cups (500 mL) all-purpose flour
½ tsp (2 mL) salt
1 tsp (5 mL) ground ginger
1 tsp (5 mL) ground cinnamon
pinch of ground nutmeg
1 tsp (5 mL) baking powder
⅔ cup (150 mL) unsalted butter, at room
    temperature
1 large egg
3 apples
whipped cream or vanilla ice cream as garnish

Preheat oven to 350°F (180°C).

Grease the sides of a 10-in (25-cm) springform pan and dust with flour. Line the bottom of the pan with parchment paper, then brush it with melted butter and sprinkle with ¼ cup (60 mL) brown sugar. Reserve.

In a saucepan over high heat, bring water to a boil; remove from heat and stir in molasses and baking soda. Allow to cool to lukewarm. In a bowl, combine flour, salt, ginger, cinnamon, nutmeg and baking powder.

Using an electric mixer on medium speed, cream together the butter and remaining brown sugar for about 3 minutes. Add egg and mix well. On low speed, slowly incorporate the flour mixture, alternating with the molasses mixture. Stir well after each addition, brushing down the sides of the bowl with a spatula.

Peel and core apples and cut into eighths. Arrange on the bottom of the prepared pan.

Pour batter over apples and bake until a toothpick inserted into the centre of the cake comes out clean, about 45 to 50 minutes. Remove from the oven and allow to cool. Carefully remove sides from the pan while cake is still slightly warm, and invert onto a serving plate.

Serve in wedges with whipped cream or ice cream.

Serves 6 to 8.

Apple Nut
Pound Cake

An ample cake that is easy to prepare, this recipe is sure to become a family favourite. Serve it by the slice at room temperature, or warmed and accompanied by ice cream.

1 tsp (5 mL) ground cinnamon
2 ⅛ cups (530 mL) granulated sugar, portioned
1 cup (250 mL) butter, softened
4 eggs
1 tsp (5 mL) vanilla
2 ⅔ cups (650 mL) all-purpose flour
1 tbsp (15 mL) baking powder
¼ tsp (1 mL) salt
¼ cup (60 mL) apple juice
4 apples, cored, peeled and sliced
⅓ cup (75 mL) chopped walnuts or pecans

Preheat oven to 325°F (160°C). Grease and flour a 10-in (25-cm) tube pan.

In a small bowl, combine cinnamon and 3 tbsp (45 mL) sugar; reserve.

With a mixer, cream butter and remaining sugar until light and fluffy. Add eggs, one at a time, beating well after each addition; add vanilla. Sift together flour, baking powder and salt, and add to batter alternately with the apple juice, mixing just until the batter is smooth.

Pour half of the batter into the tube pan. Arrange half of the apple slices and all of the nuts on top of the batter. Sprinkle half of the cinnamon sugar over the nuts and apples. Pour remaining batter in pan; top with remaining apples and sprinkle with remaining cinnamon sugar mixture.

Bake for 75 to 80 minutes or until a toothpick inserted in centre of the cake comes out clean. Cool for 15 minutes on a wire rack and then invert and cool completely.

Makes 12 generous servings.

Torta di Mele Alla Panna
(Apple Cream Pie)

La Perla, Dartmouth, NS

At La Perla they garnish this flan with a dusting of cinnamon, lemon zest and fresh mint leaves.

1 ¼ cups (300 mL) all-purpose flour
½ tsp (2 mL) salt
½ tsp (2 mL) ground cinnamon
¾ cup (175 mL) granulated sugar, portioned
1 tsp (2 mL) baking powder
2 tsp (10 mL) lemon zest
½ cup (125 mL) unsalted butter, at room
   temperature
1 egg yolk
2 tbsp (30 mL) sherry
2 large apples, peeled, cored and sliced
2 eggs
2 tbsp (30 mL) all-purpose flour (2nd amount)
¼ tsp (1 mL) salt
8 oz (250 g) cream cheese, softened
½ cup (125 mL) heavy cream (35% m.f.)
2 tsp (10 mL) lemon zest
1 tbsp (15 mL) mixed peel
¼ cup (60 mL) raisins

Preheat oven to 375°F (190°C).

Combine the flour, salt, cinnamon, ¼ cup (60 mL) sugar, baking powder and lemon zest in a large bowl. Cut in butter with a pastry blender. Beat egg yolk and sherry; pour over flour mixture and stir with a fork to incorporate. Gather dough into a ball and roll between two pieces of waxed paper to form a 10-in (25-cm) circle.

Position pastry in a 10-in (25-cm) flan pan and trim edges. Arrange apples, overlapping slightly, on the flan pastry.

Beat eggs and remaining sugar until thick and lemon-coloured. Gradually blend in salt and 2nd amount of flour. Add cream cheese in chunks and beat until smooth. Stir in cream, lemon zest, mixed peel and raisins; pour over apples.

Bake for 45 to 55 minutes. Cool, then refrigerate. Garnish with additional whipped cream sprinkled with a little cinnamon, if desired.

Serves 6 to 8.

Apple Raisin
Tart

Inn at Bay Fortune, Bay Fortune, PE

When Michael Smith was the chef at the Inn at Bay Fortune he prepared this dessert as small individual tarts. But, for the ease of the home cook, we have adjusted the recipe to fit a large 10-in (25-cm) pan.

Crust:

1 cup (250 mL) all-purpose flour
1 cup (250 mL) chopped walnuts
¼ tsp (1 mL) salt
¼ cup (60 mL) brown sugar
¼ cup (60 mL) unsalted butter, cut in chunks
1 to 1 ½ tbsp (15 to 22 mL) cold water

Combine flour, walnuts, salt and sugar in the bowl of a food processor fitted with metal blade. Pulse for about 10 seconds, being careful not to over process. Add butter chunks, and process for a few seconds. Sprinkle with water and process a few seconds longer. Press the nut crust evenly into a greased 10-in (25-cm) springform or tart pan fitted with a removable bottom. Reserve.

Filling:

1 cup (250 mL) raisins
¾ cup (175 mL) water
5 to 6 cooking apples (Cortland, Spartan, Gravenstein)
¾ cup (175 mL) apple cider
2 tsp (10 mL) ground nutmeg
1 cup (250 mL) brown sugar

Combine raisins and water in a small saucepan and simmer until all water is absorbed. Remove from heat and cool. Peel, core and slice apples into ¼-in (0.5-cm) pieces. Combine apples, raisins, cider, nutmeg and ¾ cup (175 mL) of the sugar, mixing well. Take one-half of the apple mixture, combine with remaining sugar and add to a heavy skillet. Over high heat, sauté apples to caramelize, stirring occasionally. Remove from heat and allow to cool slightly. Pour into a blender and purée to form a thick applesauce. Combine sauce with remaining filling and pour into prepared crust.

Topping:

1 cup (250 mL) rolled oats
½ cup (125 mL) brown sugar
1 ½ tsp (7 mL) ground cinnamon
2 ½ tbsp (37 mL) butter

Preheat oven to 350°F (180°C).

In a bowl, mix together oats, sugar and cinnamon. Cut in butter and blend until crumbly. Sprinkle topping over tart and bake for 40 to 50 minutes or until the filling has bubbled and the apple pieces are tender. Cool and garnish with ice cream, fresh fruit, or a sauce, if desired.

Serves 10 to 12.

Roasted Apple
and Rosemary Tart

Dalvay-by-the-Sea, Dalvay, PE

The chef at Dalvay changes his menu every three to four weeks to best reflect what is seasonally available. Utilizing fresh rosemary from the inn's kitchen garden, he has produced a delicious variation of this caramelized apple tart.

Pastry:
1 ¾ cups (425 mL) all-purpose flour
⅓ cup (75 mL) granulated sugar
½ tsp (2 mL) salt
½ cup + 1 tbsp (140 mL) softened butter
½ cup (125 mL) cold water

Sift flour, sugar and salt together in a mixing bowl. Rub butter into flour mixture until sandy in texture. Gradually add water and mix until dough is smooth but not sticky. Wrap dough in plastic wrap, refrigerate and let rest for at least 20 minutes.

Preheat oven to 375°F (190°C).

Grease and flour a 9-in (22.5-cm) springform cake pan. Roll out pastry on a floured surface to ¼-in (0.5-cm) thickness. Carefully place pastry in pan; line with foil and fill with dried beans or rice. Bake for 10 minutes or until pastry is cooked. Remove foil and beans and let cool.

Apple Filling:
⅓ cup (75 mL) melted butter
½ cup (125 mL) brown sugar
1 tsp (5 mL) ground cinnamon
1 tsp (5 mL) fresh rosemary leaves, minced
  (½ tsp/2 mL dried)
4 baking apples, peeled, cored and cut in
  wedges

Preheat oven to 375°F (190°C).

In a small bowl, combine butter, sugar, cinnamon and rosemary. Dip apple segments in butter mixture and coat well. Place apples close together on a baking sheet and bake until they are slightly softened and have caramelized, about 8 to 10 minutes. Watch apples carefully so that they do not burn. Remove from oven and cool.

Custard:
2 eggs, beaten
¾ cup (175 mL) heavy cream (35% m.f.)
½ teaspoon (2 mL) vanilla
½ cup (125 mL) granulated sugar

Preheat oven to 350°F (180°C).

Arrange apple filling on baked pastry. Whisk together eggs, cream, vanilla and sugar and pour over apples. Bake for 30 to 35 minutes, until custard is set. Remove from oven and cool. Serve alone, or with whipped cream or a favourite sauce.

Serves 8.

Apple Cranberry Crumble
with Oats and Almonds

Deerhurst Resort, Huntsville, ON

We made this dessert as our offering to a friend's Thanksgiving dinner. The response was a unanimous "Wonderful." The proof was in the fact that, even though full from turkey and all the fixings, everyone wanted seconds. Executive chef Rory Golden uses Deerhurst Resort's own maple syrup in this specialty recipe.

Filling:

½ cup (125 mL) dried cranberries
1 cinnamon stick
1 cup (250 mL) water
5 McIntosh apples, cored, peeled and thinly
   sliced
½ cup (125 mL) maple syrup
1 tsp (5 mL) lemon juice
1 tsp (5 mL) all-purpose flour

Preheat oven to 350°F (180°C). Lightly grease a deep pie plate.

In a small saucepan, combine water, cinnamon stick and cranberries; bring to a boil, reduce heat and simmer 5 minutes. Drain, remove cinnamon and pat cranberries dry.

In a bowl, toss apples, cranberries, maple syrup and lemon juice. Dust flour into apples while tossing to avoid lumping. Press apple mixture into pie plate; reserve.

Topping:

1 ½ tbsp (22 mL) all-purpose flour
2 cups (500 mL) rolled oats
¾ cup (175 mL) sliced almonds
¾ cup (175 mL) brown sugar
1 tsp (5 mL) ground cinnamon
⅓ cup (75 mL) unsalted butter, melted

In a bowl combine oats, almonds, brown sugar, flour and cinnamon. Add melted butter and mix thoroughly.

Press the crumble mixture on top of the apples and pack down to firm. Set pie plate on a baking sheet (to catch boil-over) and bake for 50 to 60 minutes, until top is browned and apples are soft; check for doneness by inserting a knife in the middle of the pie.

Pour additional maple syrup over the crumble top and serve immediately. If desired, accompany with vanilla ice cream, whipped cream or a good cheddar cheese.

Serves 6 to 8.

Apple and Almond Clafouti
with Cinnamon Cream

Acton's Grill and Café, Wolfville, NS

Originating in France, the clafouti is a pancake-style dessert traditionally made with cherries. In this version the chef at Acton's uses King or Gravenstein apples and serves the clafouti warm with Cinnamon Cream Sauce.

2 tbsp (30 mL) unsalted butter, melted
3 large apples, peeled, cored and quartered
¼ cup (60 mL) sour cream
zest from ½ lemon
½ cup (125 mL) granulated sugar
1 tbsp (15 mL) all-purpose flour
4 eggs separated
½ cup (125 mL) sliced almonds
Cinnamon Cream Sauce (recipe follows)

Grease a 2-in (5-cm) deep baking dish with melted butter. Arrange apple quarters in baking dish and reserve.

In a saucepan, over moderate heat, whisk together sour cream, lemon zest, sugar, flour and egg yolks; cook until mixture thickens slightly. Remove from heat and cool.

Preheat oven to 325°F (160°C).

Beat egg whites until stiff, but not dry, and immediately fold into the sour cream mixture. Pour cream mixture over apples and sprinkle with almonds.

Bake for 40 to 50 minutes until the clafouti is puffed and nicely browned. Serve warm with Cinnamon Cream Sauce.

Serves 6.

Cinnamon Cream Sauce:
1 cup (250 mL) heavy cream (35% m.f.)
2 tbsp (30 mL) granulated sugar
½ tsp (2 mL) ground cinnamon

In a mixer, whip the cream with the sugar and cinnamon until it begins to thicken. Serve over warm clafouti.

Makes 1 cup (250 mL) sauce.

Fuji Apple
Galette

Bishop's Restaurant, Vancouver, BC

Dennis Green, executive chef at Bishop's, finds that large Fuji apples, the size of a softball at times, are among the best varieties for tarts and pies when you want the apple to retain some texture after baking. Other good baking varieties include Gala and Spartan.

A galette is perhaps the simplest of all fruit tarts. Make it with a round of pastry which is folded over a fruit filling, leaving a small hole in the centre at the top. Chef Green suggests filling the galettes with any type of fresh fruit or berry that you would put in a pie. Simply let the fruit of the season dictate.

¼ cup (60 mL) granulated sugar
½ tsp (2 mL) ground cinnamon
pinch each of ground cardamom, cloves and
    nutmeg
¼ cup (60 mL) butter
3 Fuji apples, cored, peeled, halved diagonally
    and cut in ⅛-in (3-mm) slices
2 to 3 tbsp (30 to 45 mL) coarse raw sugar
    (Turbinado, Barbados or Demerara)
Pastry (recipe follows)

Preheat oven to 375°F (190°C) and line a baking sheet with parchment paper.

Divide pastry into 6 portions. Roll out each portion on a lightly floured surface to form a round 6 in (15 cm) in diameter.

In a bowl, combine sugar, cinnamon, cardamom, cloves and nutmeg.

Place a small dab of butter and a sprinkle of sugar mixture on each pastry round. Top each with slices from half an apple, being careful to leave an edge wide enough to fold towards the centre. Add another dab of butter and another sprinkle of sugar mixture. Fold up the pastry edges to encase the filling, leaving a hole open in the centre.

Transfer galettes to baking sheet, sprinkle raw sugar on exposed pastry. Bake in oven until pastry is golden and apples cooked, about 30 minutes. Allow to cool slightly. Serve on individual plates while still warm.

Serves 6.

Pastry:

1 ½ cups (375 mL) all-purpose flour
1 tsp (5 mL) granulated sugar
½ tsp (2 mL) salt
¾ cup (175 mL) butter, softened slightly
2 tbsp (30 mL) cold water

In a bowl, combine flour, sugar and salt. Add butter and mix until the texture becomes coarse and mealy. Add water and combine well. Knead lightly until the dough forms a ball, taking care not to overmix. Wrap in plastic wrap and refrigerate 30 minutes.

Apple
Fritters

Inn on the Lake, Waverley, NS

We used different varieties of apples to test this recipe and found each type has a distinctive flavour as well as a different cooking time. We especially enjoyed the traditional Cortland and the newer Jonagold variety.

1 cup (250 mL) all-purpose flour
1 tsp (5 mL) baking powder
2 tbsp (30 mL) granulated sugar
½ tsp (2 mL) salt
1 egg, beaten
⅔ to ¾ cup (150 to 175 mL) milk
4 to 6 apples
vegetable oil for deep frying
½ cup (125 mL) sugar (2nd amount)
1 tsp (5 mL) ground cinnamon

Sift flour, baking powder, sugar and salt into a mixing bowl. Combine beaten egg and milk and whisk into the flour mixture, using enough liquid to form a fairly thick batter. Cover, refrigerate and let batter rest for 20 minutes.

Peel, core and cut apples into ½-in (1-cm) round slices. Dip apples into batter, making sure they are well coated. Fry the slices in a deep fryer or skillet at 350° to 375°F (180° to 190°C), until the batter is golden on both sides and the apples are soft. Insert a toothpick in the apple to test for doneness. Remove from skillet and drain on paper towels.

In a bowl combine sugar (2nd amount) and cinnamon. Toss fritters in the cinnamon-sugar mixture. Serve alone, or with fresh fruit and sauce of your choice.

Serves 4 to 6.

Apple Bread Pudding
with Caramel Sauce

Pyramid Lake Resort, Jasper, AB

This "comfort food" dessert is a combination of taste sensations: the sweet-tart flavour of warm apples, the buttery richness of baked croissants, the silkiness of warm caramel sauce with cold vanilla ice cream.

1 ½ tbsp (22 mL) butter
2 Granny Smith apples, peeled, cored and thinly sliced
¼ cup (60 mL) granulated sugar
1 cup (250 mL) heavy cream (35% m.f.)
3 large eggs
6 medium or 4 large day-old croissants
Caramel Sauce (recipe follows)

In a skillet over medium heat, melt the butter and sauté the apple slices until softened and lightly caramelized, about 10 to 12 minutes. Stir 1 tbsp (15 mL) of the sugar and all the cream into the apple mixture, bring to a boil and remove from heat.

In a large bowl, whisk the eggs with the remaining sugar. Add the apple mixture to the eggs and stir to combine. Tear the croissants into bite-size pieces and stir into the egg mixture. Let the mixture rest for 30 minutes until all the liquid is absorbed.

Add pudding to a buttered 1 ½ qt (1.5 L) baking dish, cover loosely with foil and bake at 350°F (180°C) for 15 minutes. Remove foil and bake until lightly browned and firm to the touch, about 15 minutes longer.

Serve warm with ice cream and warm Caramel Sauce.

Serves 6.

Caramel Sauce:

¼ cup (60 mL) butter
1 cup (250 mL) cream (35% m.f.)
½ cup (125 mL) packed brown sugar
2 tbsp (30 mL) light corn syrup
1 tsp (5 mL) pure vanilla extract

In a small saucepan, melt butter over medium heat; add cream, sugar, corn syrup and vanilla and bring to a boil, stirring. Boil hard, stirring constantly, for 5 minutes. Let cool for 10 minutes before removing to a serving pitcher.

Makes 1 cup (250 mL).

Sticky Apple Pudding
with Toffee Sauce

Evangeline Café, Grand Pré, NS

You will simply love this creation from the chef at Evangeline Café. A cross between old-fashioned gingerbread and sticky toffee pudding, the dessert won 1st place in the annual Annapolis Valley Apple Blossom Festival dessert competition in 2005.

2 cups (500 mL) apple cider
½ cup (125 mL) chopped dates
4 tsp (20 mL) baking soda
⅓ cup (75 mL) butter, softened
1 ¼ cups (310 mL) granulated sugar
3 eggs
2 cups (500 mL) all-purpose flour
1 tbsp (15 mL) baking powder
1 tsp (5 mL) ground cinnamon
½ tsp (2 mL) each ground nutmeg and cloves
2 Cortland apples, peeled, cored and cut in ¼-in (0.5-cm) dice
Toffee Sauce (recipe follows)

Preheat oven to 350°F (180°C). Grease a 9 x 13-in (3.5-L) cake pan.

In a large saucepan, bring liquid and dates to a boil. Boil until soft, about 5 minutes. Remove from heat and stir in baking soda (mixture will froth and increase in volume). Cool.

In a mixer, cream butter and sugar until light and fluffy. Add eggs, one at a time, beating after each addition.

In a bowl, combine flour, baking powder and spices. Stir flour alternately with date mixture into the egg mixture. Stir in diced apple.

Pour batter into prepared pan and bake in oven for 40 to 50 minutes, until tester inserted in centre comes out clean. Serve warm with Toffee Sauce.

Serves 8.

Toffee Sauce:
¾ cup (175 mL) butter
1 ¼ cups (310 mL) brown sugar
¾ cup (175 mL) heavy cream (35% m.f.)
½ tsp (2 mL) vanilla

In a saucepan, melt butter over medium heat. Add sugar and stir until dissolved. Stir in cream and simmer until slightly thickened. Remove from heat and stir in vanilla. Serve warm.

Makes 1 ½ cups (375 mL).

Blomidon Baked
Apple

Blomidon Inn, Wolfville, NS

The chefs at Blomidon Inn created this variation of a conventional baked apple and it is sinfully delicious! Place seven small dots of darker-coloured sauce such as chocolate or black currant on the Crème Anglaise and, beginning at the top, run a toothpick through the dots to make a heart.

6 baking apples
¼ cup (60 mL) raisins
¼ cup (60 mL) currants
¼ cup (60 mL) chopped walnuts
¾ tsp (3 mL) ground cinnamon
¼ tsp (1 mL) ground nutmeg
¼ cup (60 mL) butter, softened
¼ cup (60 mL) brown sugar
6 sheets phyllo pastry
⅓ cup (75 mL) butter, melted (2nd amount)
Crème Anglaise (recipe follows)

Preheat oven to 375°F (190°C).

Core the apples and score the skin. Combine and mix together raisins, currants, walnuts, cinnamon, nutmeg, softened butter and sugar. Stuff raisin mixture into apples.

Brush one sheet of phyllo pastry with melted butter and then cut into six equal squares. Turn the apple upside-down on a phyllo square and fold the pastry up and around the apple.

Turn the apple upright and place the second square of pastry on and around the apple. Continue applying pastry in this fashion until all squares are used and the apple is well covered. Repeat procedure for remaining apples.

Place apples on ungreased baking sheet and bake for 20 to 30 minutes. Length of time will depend on type of apple used. Test for doneness with a toothpick; if it goes in smoothly, the apple is cooked.

To serve, place apple on large dinner plate and garnish with Crème Anglaise and mint leaves.

Serves 6.

Crème Anglaise:
½ cup (125 mL) heavy cream (35% m.f.)
½ cup (125 mL) milk
2 egg yolks
4 tbsp (60 mL) icing sugar

Heat cream and milk in the top of a double boiler over hot water. Whisk together yolks and icing sugar. Stir a small amount of the hot mixture into the yolks, return yolks to hot mixture and cook gently until mixture lightly coats the back of a spoon. Remove from heat, cover with plastic wrap and chill.

Makes 1 cup (250 mL).

A lighter version of Crème Anglaise can be made by using 1 cup (250 mL) whole milk in place of the heavy cream and milk combination.

Apple Caramel
Cheesecake

This recipe was shared a few years ago by a chef at a Dartmouth tearoom. Designed for those of us with a sweet tooth, it will become a family favourite — we promise!

Crust:

1 ½ cups (375 mL) all-purpose flour
½ cup (125 mL) butter
¾ cup (175 mL) granulated sugar
1 egg yolk

Combine flour, margarine, sugar and egg yolk. Press into the bottom and slightly up the sides of a greased 9-in (22.5-cm) springform pan; set aside.

Cheesecake:

2 tbsp (30 mL) butter
2 apples, peeled, cored and thinly sliced
20 caramels
½ tsp (2 mL) milk
1 lb (500 g) cream cheese, at room temperature (use low-fat if desired)
½ cup (125 mL) granulated sugar
2 eggs
1 tsp (5 mL) vanilla
whipped cream and additional melted caramels for garnish (optional)

Preheat oven to 325°F (160°C).

Melt butter in a skillet and sauté apples until slightly golden. Arrange apples on prepared crust.

Combine caramels and milk and melt over low heat or microwave on low power for 4 minutes. Drizzle over apples.

In a mixer, beat cream cheese and sugar until mixture is light and fluffy. Beat in eggs, one at a time; add vanilla. Pour mixture over apple-caramel mixture and bake for 35 to 40 minutes until cooked. Cool on a wire rack, then chill.

To serve: cut in wedges and garnish with additional caramel sauce and whipped cream, if desired.

Serves 10 to 12.

Château Bonne Entente
Apple Crepes

Château Bonne Entente, Sainte Foy, QC

While the chef at Château Bonne Entente included a crepe or pancake recipe, he advises that commercially prepared crepes will work as well.

Crepes:

1½ cups (375 mL) all-purpose flour
¼ cup (60 mL) granulated sugar
pinch salt
3 eggs, beaten
2 cups (500 mL) whole milk (3.25% m.f.)
2 tsp (10 mL) butter, melted
1 tbsp (15 mL) butter (2nd amount)

In a large bowl, mix the flour, sugar and salt. Combine eggs, milk and melted butter in a separate bowl and add to flour mixture, stirring only until blended. Allow batter to rest 2 to 3 hours.

Heat a crepe or omelette pan over moderate heat and melt 1 tbsp (15 mL) butter. Spoon in approximately 2 tbsp (30 mL) of batter, tipping the skillet to spread. When lightly browned, flip crepe and brown other side. Repeat this procedure until all the batter has been used, adding a little more butter, if necessary. Set aside to cool.

Filling:

4 apples, peeled, cored and sliced
¼ cup (60 mL) butter
1 cup (250 mL) pure maple syrup
⅓ cup (75 mL) granulated sugar
2 tbsp (30 mL) cornstarch, dissolved in a little cold water
1 tsp (5 mL) vanilla

Sauce:

1 cup (250 mL) heavy cream (35% m.f.)
⅓ cup (75 mL) brown sugar
1 tsp (5 mL) vanilla

Combine apple slices in a saucepan with melted butter and cook over medium heat for approximately 3 minutes, stirring occasionally. Remove pan from burner. Dissolve cornstarch and stir into maple syrup; add vanilla. Combine apples and syrup mixture and return to burner, cooking only until apples are tender and sauce has thickened. Set aside.

In a small saucepan over medium heat, bring cream and brown sugar to a boil. Reduce heat and simmer 5 minutes. Remove from heat and stir in vanilla.

Preheat oven to 325°F (160°C).

Place 2 tbsp (30 mL) apple mixture on each crepe and roll. Place crepes on a buttered ovenproof pan, drizzle with sauce, cover with aluminum foil and bake 10 minutes. Serve warm.

Makes 6 servings.

New Crop Apple Tartlet
with Quebec Rassembleu Cheese

Restaurant Les Fougères, Chelsea, QC

Chef Charles Part serves this dessert with a wedge of local Rassembleu cheese from Ste. Sophie, Quebec. Since there are no spices added to this recipe, you find only the true natural flavour of apple and cheese tantalizing your palate. Delicious!

Filling:

6 crisp, tart apples (McIntosh, Cortland, Lobo, etc.)
½ cup water

Peel, core and chop apples. Over medium-low heat, combine apples and water in a large saucepan. Bring to a simmer, reduce heat to low and cook slowly, stirring often, until apples are soft. Place apple mixture in a fine-mesh sieve and drain overnight.

Pastry:

1½ cups (375 mL) all-purpose flour
pinch of salt
¾ cup (175 mL) cold butter, cubed
⅓ cup (75 mL) cold water

In a food processor with metal blade, combine flour and salt. Add butter cubes and pulse until the texture of breadcrumbs. With the processor running, gradually add just enough cold water for the dough to form a ball. Enclose in plastic wrap and refrigerate.

Assembly:

2 additional apples
½ cup (125 mL) granulated sugar

Preheat oven to 375°F (190°C). Line a baking sheet with parchment paper.

On a floured surface roll out pastry to ¼ in (0.5 cm) thick. Cut out 6 individual 4-in (10-cm) rounds. Place rounds on the baking sheet, cover and chill for 20 minutes.

Core apples and cut in half from top to bottom. Slice apple into very thin crescent-shaped slices.

Place ¼ cup (50 mL) filling in the centre of each round. Arrange apple slices in a neat circle to enclose the filling and cover the pastry. Shake a good coating of sugar onto the tartlets.

Bake until golden and bubbly, about 20 minutes. Accompany tartlets with a wedge of Rassembleu or other fine-quality blue cheese served at room temperature.

Serves 6.

Classic
Apple Crisp

Mountain Gap Inn and Resort, Smiths Cove, NS

This easy-to-prepare dessert from Mountain Gap
Inn is a traditional Maritime favourite. Serve it
with a wedge of cheddar cheese, a scoop of
vanilla ice cream, or whipped cream.

6 to 8 apples, peeled, cored and sliced
2 tbsp (30 mL) lemon juice
¼ cup (60 mL) granulated sugar
½ cup (125 mL) butter, softened
¾ cup (175 mL) all-purpose flour
½ cup (125 mL) brown sugar
½ tsp (2 mL) ground cinnamon

Preheat oven to 350°F (180°C).

Toss apples with lemon juice and sugar and
spread in a 9-in (22.5-cm) square pan.

In a bowl, rub butter, flour, brown sugar and
cinnamon together until crumbly. Sprinkle evenly
over apples and bake until apples are tender
and the top is golden brown, about 30 to 45
minutes.

Serves 4.

Baked
Apple Delight

Quaco Inn, St. Martins, NB

Baked apples are so versatile. At the Quaco Inn the chef serves them with a scoop of rich vanilla ice cream. For a low-fat accompaniment, try frozen yoghurt.

½ cup (125 mL) golden sultana raisins
¼ cup (60 mL) brandy
5 large apples
4 tsp (20 mL) maple syrup
2 tsp (10 mL) Cointreau or other orange liqueur
2 tbsp (30 mL) granulated sugar
½ tsp (2 mL) ground cinnamon

In a small bowl, plump raisins in brandy for several hours.

Preheat oven to 375°F (190°C).

Carefully core four apples. Cut pieces from the fifth apple to fit the holes made in the bottoms of the four cored apples. Place apples in a shallow baking dish.

Fill apple cavities with plumped raisins. Pour maple syrup and Cointreau evenly over raisins. Combine sugar and cinnamon and sprinkle a teaspoon of this mixture over each apple.

Bake until tender, about 40 to 50 minutes. Test for doneness with a toothpick; if it goes in smoothly the apple is cooked.

Serves 4.

Apple
Strudel

Beild House, Collingwood, ON

According to the chefs at Beild House, this pastry is served every weekend and the guests "lap it up." Feel free to combine dried cranberries with the raisins or currants for added flavour and colour. The strudel is large (serves 10 to 12) and we froze a portion for later use. When thawed the pastry lost some of its flakiness, but was nevertheless very tasty.

Pastry:

2 cups (500 mL) all-purpose flour, portioned
¼ tsp (2 mL) salt
1 egg, beaten
½ cup (125 mL) milk
2 tsp (10 mL) melted butter

Sift 1 ½ cups (375 mL) flour and salt into a bowl; make a well. Combine egg, milk and melted butter. Add liquid to well in flour and quickly work into a soft ball of dough.

Sprinkle ½ cup (125 mL) flour on work surface. Pick up dough and throw it down on floured surface. Continue kneading in this fashion until dough is smooth and no longer sticky. Place in a bowl, tuck with a damp tea towel and let rest 1 hour.

Filling:

¾ cup (175 mL) raisins or currants
2 tbsp (30 mL) brandy or rum
1 tsp (5 mL) ground nutmeg
1 tbsp (15 mL) ground cinnamon
½ cup (125 mL) fresh bread crumbs
zest of 1 lemon
1 cup (250 mL) granulated sugar
½ cup (125 mL) chopped nuts
6 Granny Smith apples, peeled, cored and cut in ¼-in (0.5-cm) dice

In a small microwave-proof bowl, combine raisins and brandy. Cover with plastic wrap, vent and microwave for 30 seconds. This will 'plump' the fruit. Cool.

In a large bowl, combine all ingredients.

Assembly:

½ cup (125 mL) all-purpose flour
½ cup (125 mL) melted butter, portioned

Preheat oven to 400°F (200°C). Grease a baking sheet.

Sprinkle flour on a cotton-sheet-covered work table. Roll out the dough with a rolling pin using the flour to ensure that it does not stick. Roll as far as you can until very thin.

Brush the dough with butter and spread the filling to within 1 in (2.5 cm) of edges. Pick up the edge of the sheet and let the strudel roll itself up. Tuck in the ends and transfer to the baking sheet, seam side down. If necessary, form into a crescent shape to fit on the baking sheet.

Brush with butter and bake for 20 minutes. Lower heat to 350°F (180°C), brush again with butter and continue baking until golden, about 15 minutes.

Serve either warm or cold. If desired, garnish with vanilla ice cream or whipped cream.

Makes 10 to 12 servings.

Index

Photo Credits

Cover: Meghan Collins

All interior photos by Steven Isleifson, except where noted below:
Julian Beveridge: pages 22, 29, 54, 59; Gary Castle: pages 4, 7, 8, 9,10, 11, 12, 14 (all photos except Crabapple and Golden Russet), 15 (photos 2, 3, 4, 7); Ted Coldwell: pages 1, 38, 43, 57, 77, 93; Meghan Collins: pages 2, 21, 25, 30, 35, 45, 61, 67; Elena Elisseeva: pages 14 (Crabapple), 58; Marianne Fitzgerald: p.15 (McIntosh); Janet Kimber: pages 3, 33, 41, 60; Mel Lee: page 19; Virginia Lee: page 63; Terry Manzo/David Smiley/Dwayne Coon: page 50; Catherine Oakeson: page 53; Newton Page: page 15 (Spartan); Amanda Rohde: page 15 (Granny Smith); John Sigler: page 15 (Rome Beauty); Keith Vaughan: pages 6, 14 (Golden Russet), 15 (Ida Red and Northern Spy).